SMARTER
than you think!

SMARTER
than you think!

ASSESSING and PROMOTING your CHILD'S MULTIPLE INTELLIGENCES

CLAIRE GORDON & LYNN HUGGINS-COOPER

CARROLL & BROWN LIMITED

First published in 2012 in the United Kingdom by

Carroll & Brown Limited
20 Lonsdale Road
London NW6 6RD

Text © Serif Ltd 2004 and Lynn Huggins-Cooper 2005
Illustrations and compilation © Carroll & Brown Limited 2005 and 2012

A CIP catalogue record for this book is available from the British Library.

ISBN 978-1-907952-27-2

10 9 8 7 6 5 4 3 2 1

Printed in China

CONTENTS

A NEW LOOK AT INTELLIGENCE

Learning does not just happen in formal 'teaching' sessions, nor is writing things on paper proof that learning has taken place – far from it! Your child experiences things everywhere you go. She is like a sponge, soaking up the sights, sounds, smells, feelings and tastes she encounters.

Up until the 1980s, it was generally held that there was only one kind of intelligence, and that it was fixed at the same level at birth throughout our lives – our so-called IQ or intelligence quotient. In 1983, however, Harvard education professor, Howard Gardner, published his groundbreaking book, *Frames of Mind: The Theory of Multiple Intelligence*. After extensive research, Gardner proposed that there are seven different types of intelligence, and that these can be developed, challenging the view that intelligence can be summed up in one IQ score.

Gardner always maintained that although he initially found seven intelligences that fitted his strict scientific criteria, there were probably more. He has since recognised Naturalistic Intelligence (Nature Smart), for example.

Multiple intelligence theory is a positive and inclusive model of intelligence, which takes account of all the gifts we have, not just the 'academic' ones. It makes sense of the fact that there are many people whose success lies outside of the traditional intelligence framework, like concert pianists or Olympic athletes.

MULTIPLE INTELLIGENCE THEORY

In short, the theory holds that we are all smart in different ways although some more than others, that we can develop our intelligence and use it for self improvement, and that there is a framework for learning and developing that plays to our individual strengths.

Everyone possesses all the different intelligences to some degree or another. All children, for example, have the ability to be musical but some will grow up able to compose, while others will become singers and/or musicians and the majority will just love to listen to or dance to music throughout their lives. And, if given the necessary encouragement and instruction, most children can become reasonably competent in every intelligence. Because Multiple Intelligence Theory holds that one is not stuck with the intelligence profile he was born with, once you understand your child's intelligence strengths, you can help your child use them to his advantage. By working on hisweaknesses, you also help your child improve. There are many ways to be smart in each intelligence; for example, even though your child may not yet be able to read, if he or she is a good storyteller, your child is linguistically intelligent.

Intelligences do not exist in isolation; they are always interacting with each other in complex ways. A professional footballer, for instance, needs his spatial and bodily-kinesthetic intelligences to coordinate and interact if he is to pass the ball accurately.

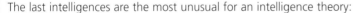

WHAT ARE THE MULTIPLE INTELLIGENCES?

To begin with, there are the two intelligences you are probably already familiar with, because they are measured in school as IQ:

Logical-Mathematical – the ability to use numbers effectively, and to deduce, reason and apply logic. In this book, these abilities are covered in Number Smart and Thinking Smart.
Linguistic – the capacity to use words effectively in speaking or writing. This is also known as Word Smart.

There are four specialist intelligences:
Musical – capability in perceiving, transforming and expressing musical forms, also called Music Smart.
Spatial – skill in perceiving and manipulating objects or images, which is also known as Picture Smart.
Bodily-Kinesthetic – physical expertise in using one's body for expression or to produce things (Body Smart).
Naturalistic This is defined as the ability to recognize and classify plants, animals and natural phenomena (Nature Smart).

The last intelligences are the most unusual for an intelligence theory:
Intrapersonal – the ability to understand and manage one's own feelings (Self Smart), and
Interpersonal – the ability to understand and manage the feelings of others (People Smart).

LEARNING STYLES

Much has been written – and millions spent – on research into learning styles. There are many theories and many different labels for the wide variety of styles that exist. It is not important to identify your child's preferred style of learning in order to label her and teach her in one particular way, but it is important to be aware that there are different styles. Most people exhibit a combination, with one tending to be stronger, and both teaching and learning are most effective when a variety of styles are used.

It is important to discover what works for your child so that you can help her to learn. By understanding your child's learning style, it will easier to teach her concepts in a way that she can readily digest. Instead of attempting to label your child, consider which broad description is closest to your child's learning style. You will have to observe her quite closely to decide. Once you have decided, you can tailor the activities to suit your child's preferred style. That being said, it is important to recognise your own preferred learning style to avoid overemphasising 'your' waywhen offering your child strategies for learning. As in many other aspects of life, your way may not be your child's way!

WHAT ARE THE LEARNING STYLES?

Auditory learner

Does your child learn easily from listening to instructions and is a good talker? If she is spelling a word does she tend to sound it out phonetically? She may learn best as an auditory learner – listening and digesting facts and directions. Language-orientated learners think in words rather than pictures, and verbalise concepts as they make sense of ideas. Children with this preferred learning style may excel at foreign language learning, as well as being potentially musically gifted.

Visual learner

Does your child remember images and diagrams? Can he recall movies, talking about different shots when he is describing his favourite part of the film? Does he enjoy drawing and like visual puzzles such as mazes? Is he a bit of a daydreamer? If your child remembers things he has seen rather than things he has heard, he may be a visual learner. As he learns to read, it is especially important to suggest visual clues. He will devour picture books but will also enjoy 'chapter books' if he is encouraged to visualise the story like a film playing in his head. Story writing can be encouraged in the same way.

Kinetic learner

Is your child's learning style firmly grounded in the physical? Is she highly active, and does she find it hard to sit still? Does your child emphasise her speech with large, whole body movements and gestures? Does she show you things rather than explain them? If so, she may be a kinetic learner. Physical activity is the key for this type of child. She will want her whole body to be involved in learning, so teach her to count by physically taking steps. and when reading, let her tap out rhythms, walk about or rock and jiggle. It sounds odd, but it really works. Don't constrain your child but be prepared to think outside the box! Kinetic learners enjoy hands-on activities and may be gifted at sports and creative thinking. A child who prefers this style of learning may find school life difficult and may easily become labelled as exhibiting signs of attention deficient disorder.

Logical learner

Does your child like to find patterns and work out relationships between objects and ideas? Does he enjoy finding out about how things work? Does he drive you insane with the amount of why-based questions he asks? Does he like maths and playing strategy games? He may be a predominantly logical learner. Hold your child's interest by carrying out science experiments together and encourage your child to explore any hypothesis he has about the science he is investigating. Do not 'give' him the answers; allow him to test his own hypotheses and draw his own conclusions.

HOW TO USE THIS BOOK

Smarter Than You Think! consists of tests and learning activities. The tests enable you to assess your child's various abilities while the activities help you to promote the development of the various intelligences. You may want to work through the tests and activities in a consistent way or simply let your child pick out those (from a pre-selected handful and have some influence over the activity undertaken), that he or she thinks look interesting and fun to do. A child who 'buys in' to a test or activity, will be enthusiastic, interested and engaged, and will naturally perform better, so you will get a clearer and more accurate picture of his or her strengths. Full instructions are included with each test or activity.

At the back of the book, you will find some Record Sheets. If you like, you can use them to note down how well your child performed each test or activity or to record his or her progress if a test or activity is done more than once.

THE TESTS

Schools increasingly use tests as a way to find out more about their students. Initially, testing may form part of the selection process, then it can help allocate children to appropriate classes, and later it may be used for monitoring progress. But you also can use tests to understand your child and to promote self-development. You (and your child) may want to know what your child's talents are so that they can be developed or why your child finds some things easy and others difficult or whether a particular learning style might make it easier for your child to learn.

THE ACTIVITIES

Both at home and further afield, there are opportunities for learning and to help develop the various intelligences. The activities enable your child to learn things in fun-filled ways. They are experiential and hands-on, so your child learns by doing and because they are active, your child will be able to remember the things he or she learns. But before you attempt the tests or activities, consider whether your home supports learning, how to use your environment to introduce exciting ideas and concepts, and what things you can do generally to engage your child's interests.

CREATING THE ENVIRONMENT TO LEARN

Ensuring that your home and some of the things in it will stimulate your child's imagination and development is not difficult to do. Neither is making use of the different places you regularly or just occasionally visit.

THE LEARNING HOME
Every home has the potential for maximising a child's development intellectually, physically and spiritually. A few adaptations may be necessary but generally not a lot of new equipment. What you already have around the home can be put to good use as teaching aids.

The Kitchen
This room is the hub of the house and of home learning! It is the ideal science lab with access to heat, water, freezer and food materials. Food can teach your child about changing states such as freezing and melting and how solids, liquids and gases are different; it can be used to demonstrate healthy eating. The kitchen also offers maths activities, particularly lessons about capacity as you weigh and measure ingredients for cooking. *See activity cards 57, 58 and 60.*

Food can create the basis for geography lessons, as you talk about the different parts of the world the food comes from and what the climate is like there – is it different from the climate where you live, and does that affect what will grow?

Learning to use a recipe teaches children about instructional writing. They discover that it has a particular format – ingredients followed by method, and that it gives information needed to carry out a task. It also teaches about the importance of chronology in writing; if we don't follow the recipe in the right order, we can end up with some odd results! Writing recipes is also good practice in 'writing for a purpose'.

The Bathroom
This is the perfect place for exploring floating and sinking; 'soap science' with bubbles; volume and the way liquids change shape to fill a vessel, and how water and soap makes things slippery – a discovery about reducing friction! With the aid of a couple of jugs or other graduated containers, bath time can become a maths lesson about capacity and volume. *See activity cards 56.*

Bathing is a good time in which to stimulate language development. While washing, your child can make up bubble poems; tell stories about shipwrecks, mermaids and pirates and even think of musical sea shanties with an orchestra of water-filled containers to bash, rattle and blow. *See activity card 56.*

The Living Room
The living room often contains the television and DVD player. These aren't necessarily bad for children; what is bad is the lack of conversation and the encouragement of passivity. Make sure you spend time watching and discussing programmes with your child. Together, try to think of spin-off activities from a favourite programme. For example, your child could make a cartoon character's bedroom using a carton and junk modelling. Make sure you ask your child why he has chosen the items he has to make his model. This way it also becomes a lesson in technology, art and characterisation all in one.

Either here or in your child's room is a good place for a cosy book corner. All you need are a few cushions and a plastic crate full of a changing selection of books (rotating books from your child's bookshelves or from the library) will encourage your child to take pleasure in reading (*see also page 13*). You should encourage your child to make a themed display each week for her favourite book: for example, a collection of postcards, plastic bugs or puppets to accompany Alien Invaders, a rubber frog and tadpole set for Frog's Diary, etc.

The Dining Room

A wipeable mat can transform the average dining table into an arts and crafts station. Even if your table is a valuable antique, it can still serve as a den with the help of cloths flung across the top, cushions underneath and dressing-up accessories. It can become a cave ... an igloo ... the basement of a haunted mansion ... wherever your child's interests lie. *See activity 53.* The dining room also is, of course the best place to learn the art of conversation. Make sure, even with differing schedules, that you eat together several times a week, setting the table properly with your child's help.

The Bedroom

Everybody – adult or child – needs a calm, contemplative space to be himself and to collect his thoughts. A bedroom can provide this. Adequate storage makes toys easier to get out and clear away, and giving your child open access to toys and art equipment helps to spark off ideas for activities, avoiding the dreaded 'I'm bored'!

Marking boxes with labels your child has made on the computer will help boost

her information technology skills, and turn her room into a more literate environment at a stroke.

The Garden

This is a priceless resource for learning. Apart from active play on swings, slides, frames, etc., to boost fitness and health, the garden is a great place for open-ended, discovery-based learning. Even the youngest child will enjoy messing with sand, water, dry leaves, and clean compost.

The garden is a wonderful place for the safe exploration of the natural world and its biology. Here a child can watch plants grow, enjoy bug and bird behaviour, look at rocks and soils, study weather and possibly explore pond life. *See activity cards 31 and 32.*

Wonderful dens can be constructed cheaply and easily from bought tents, sheets and chairs or, as in our garden, from natural materials. A willow tepee, tunnel or dome can be built easily by pushing willow rods into the ground and keeping them watered and weed free for a year as they establish. The screen formed by the sprouting leaves allows the child to feel enclosed, but also allows you to feel secure as you can see your child as she plays. The structure can be interwoven with climbers such as sweet peas, clematis or jasmine for scent and extra interest or with edible crops such as peas or beans.

Turf 'tuffets' or seats are easily made by filling a circle of fresh willow sticks, stuck into the ground. The circle is filled with soil before being capped with turf or low-growing herbs such as prostrate rosemary or chamomile treneague, which give off a delicious scent as they are crushed – or sat on. These 'pixie seats' can be made in a companionable circle and a fairy grotto can be constructed from twigs or willow, and hung with crystals and wind chimes for enchanting role play adventures.

Try to garden together with your child and talk to him about what you are doing – and why. If possible, give your child his own patch to cultivate. Plant fruit and vegetables as well as flowers, as children love to consume what they grow. Talk about the way a plant grows from a seed – even a huge tree. Ask your child if he knows what a green plant needs to grow healthily, such as light and water. See activity cards:

Talk about how soil is made, and then make compost together to demonstrate. Think about keeping a wormery, with brandling (fishing bait) worms, to demonstrate the way worms work in the soil to break down organic matter. You get a bonus of rich plant food into the bargain!

YOUR MAKE AND GLUE KIT

- Apron
- Scissors (age-appropriate)
- Ruler
- Tape: clear plastic and masking
- Glue: glue sticks, PVA glue, glue pot and spreader
- Pens: felt-tip, gel pens
- Markers
- Pencils
- Eraser
- Paper: plain white, lined and coloured art
- Scrap card

USEFUL 'TOOLS' AND EQUIPMENT FOR LEARNING

To make your home a developmental environment, it's important to have a stock of art materials on hand.

Art materials

These don't have to be expensive; many are found, cast-off or reused. But, for starters, you should have on hand a make-and-glue kit (see box).

Paints need not be expensive. You can buy powder paints that you mix yourself, or ready mix. Look in discount bookshops for inexpensive boxes of oils, water colours and acrylics. Solid blocks of paint are a good option for younger children. Offer a variety of brush sizes, including fine ones. Wax crayons (both chubby and finer tipped), pencil crayons for shading and felt tips with a variety of nibs will give your child the opportunity to create many different effects. Metallic pens, chalks, pastels and gel pens are also great additions to her art kit.

Clay and other mouldable materials – dough, fimo, etc. – can be a great way for your child to explore different media and techniques, and he can use these materials to make long-lasting artifacts.

Paper can be as inexpensive or costly as you like. Computer printouts, off-cuts of wallpaper, etc., all can be used as well as more expensive 'art' paper. You also should have a store of some thicker card.

Pictures cut from magazines as well as scraps kept from packaging are also useful for collaging. Make sure you have plenty of newspaper on hand to cover surfaces. An offcut of oilcloth is also a useful protective table cover.

Beads, sequins, glitter, ribbon scraps, coloured wool and fabric remnants can all be put to good use for collaging as can pasta shapes and natural materials such as leaves, flowers, pine cones, acorns, seed pods, grasses, shells and feathers.

Packaging is of great benefit for the various projects in the book. Quite a number of normal household items such as egg cartons, toilet roll inserts, bubble wrap, ice cream and yoghurt tubs, tissue roll centres, netting from fruit packaging and tissue and cereal boxes can be used for 'junk modelling' and art activities. A toilet roll insert covered in a few layers of papier mâché and given a base, can be decorated to look like a space rocket, a drinks can, a lighthouse – whatever your child fancies!

Storage

Once you have collected all of these useful items, you need somewhere to store them.

Keeping them organised can be as simple and cheap as you want.

Large plastic crates are available very cheaply from bargain stores, but large cardboard cartons decorated by your child will do the job just as well – and making them is an activity in itself. Your child could paint the cartons with paint plus a little PVA glue mixed in for durability and shine. Or together you can glue on pictures either drawn by your child or cut from comics, etc. covered with a layer of PVA that will dry clear to the sides and top.

Paper files can be made from empty cereal packets. Cut the top off the box diagonally, paint and decorate it in a style of your choice.

Plastic tool boxes or shoe holders (the type with pockets that hangs on the wall) are cheap to buy and great for holding crayons, erasers and smaller 'found objects'. If your child can see where things are, she is more likely to use them.

Cutlery trays can be used to store paintbrushes and pens, and small plastic indoor rubbish bins can be used to store bulkier items such as wool, fabrics, etc.

Books

Fostering a love of books and reading is possibly the greatest gift you can offer your child. Books are the key to different worlds, times and places and the single-most important 'toy' you can give your child. Being able to access the knowledge held in non-fiction books means your child can find a solution to many of the questions he or she has about the world, and the challenges he or she may encounter. Reading fiction offers a world of mind-expanding ideas to your child.

To love books, a child needs to be comfortable with them and to see them as a source of pleasure. Research has shown that the best way to encourage reading right from the beginning is to create a literate environment. Make sure your child sees adults and older children reading for pleasure and he or she will see it as something natural. Create labels for toy boxes, etc., and point out print in the environment, such as signs and notices. A great way to encourage your child is to make books together (*see also page 20*).

It is important that your child has his or her own home library. If you cannot afford to buy many new books, scour second-hand or charity shops; they often have a good selection of children's books. You also can join a library and a book club.

Expose your child to a wide variety of books, fiction and non-fiction. Comic books and graphic novels have their place, too. Offer your child stories from other cultures, traditional tales, myths and legends, poetry, and colourful information filled books.

Imaginative toys

There are so many brightly coloured, beautifully packaged toys and games on the market that it can be hard to decide what to buy although certain types of toys should be included in every household.

Construction toys can include bricks that can be joined together and a variety of other linkable pieces. Kits make great presents; types that can be added to are best. Large, plastic, linkable pieces are ideal for younger children; as your child develops he'll find smaller pieces, including motors, switches and lights easier to manage.

Outdoor activity toys such as scooters, skates and bicycles are fun and give your child an opportunity to get fit and let off steam.

If you have a garden, install a sandpit and water tray, together with 'super soaker' guns. These are useful for children, as not only are they fun but can be used for many 'science' experiments, such as floating and sinking and hydraulics. If you do not have a garden area, offer your child a bowl full of play sand or water on a plastic sheet.

Dressing up clothes including hats, scarves, costume jewellery, bags can be begged from friends and relatives or bought from charity shops to supplement a dressing-up chest of commercially bought outfits. Young children enjoy role play and dressing up; older children will enjoy dressing up tied into history topics such as pirates, Romans, explorers, etc.

Every home should have a collection of puppets and even a small puppet theatre (or a cardboard box made into a theatre). These toys help to develop language skills, imagination and storytelling, and can be used to help your child to explore issues that she is having trouble articulating, such as problems with friendship, loss, etc. Using the puppet to 'speak' removes the child a degree from the things she says, and can make her feel safer about voicing her problems.

OTHER LEARNING ENVIRONMENTS

Learning does not just happen in formal 'teaching' sessions. Your child experiences things everywhere you go. She is like a sponge, soaking up the sights, sounds, smells, feelings and tastes she encounters. You may think you just are going for a simple day out, but to your child, all outings are rich in incidental learning. You can integrate learning into many family day trips if you think about it briefly before you go. Careful though: don't make it hard work (for you or your child) or you will suck all the pleasure out of them.

Wherever you are, get into the habit of talking about what you see. Ask your child open-ended questions about what she sees: 'What if …', 'Why do you think …', and be prepared for the many questions your child asks you! Never be afraid to say you don't know the answer; if you encourage her to help you 'explore' by sitting next to you while you use books and the Internet to find out answers, you will be teaching her a vital lesson: how to carry out research.

Supermarkets

Whenever and wherever you shop, talk about what you are buying and about the places the food came from. Can your child see any clues? Look at labels on packaging, stickers or in-store displays. Ask questions about food grown in different countries – why does a particular plant (such as a banana or pineapple tree) grow in one country but not another? And how do exotic fruits and vegetables get from where they grow to where you live? Who grows them? Then buy some produce that is grown abroad and when you get it home, have a tasting session and look in an atlas to find out more about where the fruit or vegetable grows.

Talk about the colours of fresh food – is strawberry red the same as cherry red? Which is more orange coloured – an

orange or a tangerine? How many 'green' vegetables can your child name.

Can you find any food you have not tried before? Talk about it and try to guess what it will taste like, then go home and see who was right!

Look for 'Fair Trade' marks on food. What does this mean? How does fair trade affect the lives of growers and suppliers? You can point out organic labels on various items. Does your child know what organic means? Why does she think people buy organic food? Could you grow any yourself?

Forests, beaches, pools and ponds

Science and the natural world are everywhere you look. Use a walk in a forested area to identify trees, leaves, plants and bugs using simple guidebooks. Make a collection of items such as leaves, nuts, feathers and stones for your child to give a 'show and tell' presentation to family at home. The materials also can be made into collages or dream catchers.

If the leaves are changing colour, find out why that happens together and make sure you collect leaves for your leaf diary (*see activity card 36*). Look for other seasonal signs if that's applicable.

The beach, like many other outdoor environments, is rich in opportunities for hands-on, experiential learning. For example, there's maths – estimating volume, measuring and looking at shapes – when you construct a sandcastle together. Even history can be introduced as you discuss fortification and dig a moat.

Ask your child to look at any pebbles and sand; talk about how the wave action changes one into the other. What is rock made into, and why is rock chosen as the material to make those things? (strength, durability, etc..)

When you walk along the beach, look at plants and creatures on the shore, and then go rock pooling. Are there different creatures in different zones on the beach?

You also can encourage language play by making up lists of sea-related things. Create a game: 'In my treasure chest I found …' and make up poetic and outrageous things such as 'a mermaid's song' or 'a pirate's smelly sock' as well as south sea pearls and jewel-encrusted daggers – it's not just a memory game; it's about stretching the imagination – and this is something that only expands with regular use.

Make up silly poems and songs, encouraged by practising alliteration (words that start with the same sound like 'salty sea' or 'rough rocks'). Give your child

examples such as 'sticky starfish' and 'wild waves'. If your child is young, you don't have to tell her it is alliteration – just tell her you are looking for descriptions that start with the same sounds. Encourage your child to find an alliterative description for seaweed, sand, fish … whatever you can see or imagine.

Apart from the excellent exercise swimming provides, a day at the pool can be a science lesson, too. Talk about floating and sinking, demonstrating with swimming floats and rings. Ask your child to float, and talk about what causes buoyancy. A walk round a pond can turn into a science trip. Bring a small net and a white dish and look closely at the plants and creatures you find before returning the creatures to the water. Talk about food chains – how they all start with the sun; green plants follow, then herbivores (plant eating creatures) and finally carnivores (meat eaters). Point out that there are 'top predators', too – carnivores that eat other, smaller carnivores (a mink eating a frog would be an example). Back at home you could make food chain drawings. You also could think about the creatures at the pond that undergo metamorphosis, such as frogs, toads, newts, dragonflies etc.

If you take a sketch pad and crayons to the pond, your child can make pictures of the changing colours seen in reflections in the water. You could write a pond poem together, and if you make it onomatopoeic, the words you use will suggest the things you are describing – 'sloppy slime; oozing mud' would be an example as it suggests sludginess! *See activity cards 34, 35 and 36.*

Museums and art galleries

Use a museum trip to find out more about a subject that really grips your child – be that bugs, dinosaurs, space travel – whatever. Think about questions you

would like to research before you go, and play detective once you are there. For example, if you go to an exhibition about dinosaurs, focus on a particular area of thought – perhaps the colour of dinosaurs. How do we know what colour they were? What evidence is there? See activity cards:

When you visit an art gallery, take a sketchbook. Your child (of whatever age; even a four- year-old can manage this) can make sketches of exhibits she likes. Sketches make a touching addition to an album of photos from trips. Can your child tell you why she does – or doesn't – like a particular exhibit? Encourage her ideas, telling her there is no right or wrong answer. Talk about tone, colour and shading to give your child access to artistic language. Take some coloured pencils, charcoals or a pack of pastels and a pad, and your child can be just like the other (albeit older) art students and artists thronging the gallery.

Public gardens

A visit to any public garden with a glasshouse offers the opportunity to think about different habitats around the world, such as a tropical rainforest or desert. This can lead to a discussion of different places in the world, and what can be found there (geography); a discussion of which plants and creatures live in different habitats, and how they are adapted (science); it also can offer the creative stimulus needed to go home and make a model 3D garden in a box or write a story about desert creatures – or make a jungle adventure board game – let your child's imagination fly freely, and take video footage and photos to refresh her memory once she is at home.

Historic site visits

When you visit a heritage site, make the history come to life by imagining what it would have been like to live at the time of the site – be it Roman remains, an old settler town or a Victorian mansion. Discuss how life was different then, compared to today. What sort of jobs did

people have, what did they wear? You can collect items to dress up as people from the time once you get home – a shawl or a cap helps a child to feel 'Victorian', a toy sword and shield can make him feel 'Roman' – as can a sheet draped as a toga! Your child can role play at home – or imagine what it would be like to time travel back to the era. See activity cards:

Farms

A visit to a farm can offer information about animal lifecycles such as 'Do the babies at the farm look like their mothers?' 'What do the animals eat?' 'Are they herbivores or carnivores – or even omnivores (eating both meat and plants)?'

What do animals need to stay healthy? (food, water, shelter). Where does our food come from and how is it produced? Many children, particularly urban dwellers, are unable to make connections between the plants or animals and the food that arrives on their plates.

DISPLAYS

Displays can be used in two ways: to showcase work and as a stimulus to promote learning. The best displays are a combination of the two. Displaying your child's work gives her the message that her work is valued, and that will boost her self-esteem.

The kitchen is a good place for displays of all types including number lines, 'word of the week' vocabulary builders and art cards as well as your child's work. If your child sees a thing regularly, this will help him to retain information.

You can put up a simple washing line display. An actual washing line or any other strong cord should be attached to the wall firmly – art work in quantity can get quite heavy! Clothes pegs – bought decorative pegs or plain wooden ones that your child can decorate with felt pens – can be used to add items to the line. If space is at a premium, fridge magnets may be useful in keeping some of these items in view of your child.

Presentation can make a great difference to displayed work. Special pieces could be mounted on coloured card, so a border shows around the edge of the artwork. Use a glue stick to attach the artwork to the card, as wet glue can make the paper pucker. Very special work can be double mounted.

Encourage your child to mount and display her own work too. This will give her ownership of the process and will help to build her self confidence.

Work can also be pasted into a book, such as a scrapbook (*see also page 20*). You could make your own display book from pieces of paper stapled or stitched down the middle to make a centre fold. The cover can be decorated and the book can be hung from ribbon or cord. Encourage your child to make displays of

objects associated with any area she is finding out more about. If she is, for example, learning about frogs, she could make a display on a coffee table by draping green fabric or a scarf and adding frog themed objects. Cuddly toys, plastic models, books and pictures as well as examples of her own work would be suitable for inclusion. Encourage her to make a label for each item and a title for the display – perhaps in bubble writing or another decorated script. This helps to create a literate environment.

Home-made books

When you make books with your child, start simply and be guided by his stage of development. As you make the books together, you will be using language skills, research skills, maths, graphic design and layout and technology. The end result will be a book that is as unique as the child who created it and can be displayed as a family keepsake, or even made to be given as a gift.

SCRAPBOOKING

A fun, creative activity, scrapbooking is something children can enjoy. Your child's scrapbook can be used as a special place for thoughts, stories or pictures, for expressing feelings, or to record a particular event such as a woodland walk or a visit to the seashore (see 'boxed' examples).

To make the cover of a bought scrapbook special, encourage your child to collage it with appropriate pictures and found objects.

LIFT-THE-FLAP BOOKS

These are easy to make and great fun! They also can contain surprises such as secret maps, pockets for treasure and tiny envelopes for storage. Envelopes are simply made by cutting a square out of paper. Draw a cross through the centre of the square going from corner to corner. Fold each corner of the square in to the centre. Put tape or a sticker in place to hold three corners together at the centre; the fourth corner is the 'flap' to be opened.

Lift-the-flap books can be enjoyed by very young children. They may be as simple as a repeated idea: 'What's under the stone?' (a series of drawings by the child about bugs) or 'What's in the rockpool?' (a series of pictures of crabs, small fish, etc.).

Older children will enjoy making envelopes themselves to stick inside their books for more sophisticated versions. You should encourage your child to secrete a small 'treasure' in each envelope and to write a 'clue' on the outside for other readers to solve.

WOODLAND WALK

Make a scrapbook with a difference to describe what you might see on in woodland. Use found items such as small twigs, leaves, seed pods, etc., as embellishments.

Page one could say something along the lines of, 'We walked in the woods – what do you think we saw?' Page two could have a drawing, collage or embellishments behind a card flap, taped down one side. This is the 'window' that the reader lifts to see the answer. For a small child it could just be 'leaves'; an older child could use more description, such as 'shiny copper leaves falling from the sky like rain' – just appeal to his imagination!

SHAPE STORYBOOK

If your child loves to listen to stories and play 'make believe', you may have a budding author on your hands! It is said in writing manuals that to be able to write a good book, one must have first served an apprenticeship reading many, many books. Give your child a head start by encouraging her storytelling, and turn her words into a shaped storybook.

The story can be about anything that your child has a passion for. It could be pirates, space travel, fairies, ghosts (or mummies, *see activity card 51*).

Encourage your child to plan her story a little. Don't force the issue and take the joy and spontaneity out of the process, but encourage your child to think about the following things and then write down the story for her:

- What is the story about? All that is needed here is a one line synopsis, just to focus the mind.
- Where does most of the action take place?
- Who are the main characters? What are they like? How do they look/talk/walk/dress?
- Is there a problem to solve in the story? Do the main characters have a challenge to overcome?
- An exciting first sentence so readers will want to read more.
- A strong ending. Make sure the problems are solved and the challenges faced! Encourage your child not just to end with 'and then they went to bed'!

After writing it down, read it through to your child. Is it what she wants to say? Are there any more exciting descriptions she could use? Once it's finished, she should choose a shape that suits her story. If it is

SEASHORE SCRAPBOOK

The book could contain tiny shells, pressed shoreline flowers, sprinkled sand and dried seaweed.

To dry seaweed, choose a non-fleshy type such as sea lettuce, or a frondy corralina as the types with pods tend to retain a smell. Lay the seaweed in a dish of clean water. Place a piece of thick cartridge or kid's craft paper underneath the seaweed, in the water. Carefully lift the weed with the paper so it lays on the paper. Put the paper somewhere to dry, but out of direct sunlight. In a few days it is dry and does not smell! Cut around the weed, and perhaps write the name or the date collected on the paper in brown ink to give the effect of a botanical sample.

Stick the seaweed, together with other shoreline treasures, to the cover of the scrapbook. Add a little vegetable netting to look like a fishing net, and randomly glue gun a few glass pebbles (the type found in candle shops) to the cover as 'sea glints'.

about a spooky old house, she could make the book in that shape. Encourage her to make a cover from layers of card, and perhaps have a tiny tissue ghost poking out of a window. If the book is about whales – she can make it whale shaped!

Once she's finished the cover, help her cut pages using the cover shape as a template and drawing round it. Use a hole punch and thread through the holes to hold the book together at the spine, or staples – but make sure you cover the staples with tape to avoid scratching little hands.

The Tests

The tests are designed as a development tool and should not be used to push your child to achieve a certain level or performance criteria. Just have fun spending time together! They vary in format and approach, as well as content. Some can be done with only a pencil and paper, others require more in the way of materials. The answer structure varies, too. Some tests have right and wrong answers, while others, such as the 'people' tests, act as springboards for discussions between you and your child, and you will need to interpret his responses based on his ability to think independently, his enjoyment of the task, and his understanding of the subject matter.

Interpreting the tests

You will get a much broader picture of your child's strengths if you do all the tests in a section. There are lots of ways to be smart in a particular area and 'Word smart', for example, has word and letter puzzles, and looks at written as well as spoken language. When you come to interpret your child's score or ability for a test, think about her performance as a whole. Are you confident she understood the task completely? Did she concentrate and really engage in what she was doing? Was she tired or distracted? These are factors that can adversely affect performance. Most importantly, did your child enjoy it – children usually like the things they are good at.

Background

Along with information on each intelligence type and test, you will find guidance on administering and assessing each one and, sometimes, suggestions as to clues and how to extend some of the activities. You will also find 'boosting tips' at the end of each test, which can be used both to stretch your child if he has performed strongly as well as to give extra help to your child if he needs it.

WHAT IS THINKING SMART?

If you imagine your mind as a muscle, then, just as you use the muscles in your legs in various ways to walk, run or jump, so, too, can your brain be used for different purposes. Thinking smart is the ability to harness your thoughts and put them to these different uses.

There are several ways of thinking, and the exercises found in this section test the three main processes:

- **Logical thinking** is the discipline of using step-by-step reasoning to see the patterns in a problem and find a rational solution to it. This involves considering possibilities, assessing information, and deciding on the most likely solution. In everyday life we use experience and knowledge to aid logical thinking.

- **Creative thinking** is almost the opposite of logical thinking. Rather than finding just one solution to a problem, with creative thinking you generate as many solutions as possible, without appraising them. This gives your mind freedom to explore, rather than following a strict route. Thinking creatively may feel counter-intuitive, as we are taught to be logical from a young age.

- **Abstract thinking** has similar principles to logical thinking, as they are both forms of reasoning. However, abstract thinking involves coding and decoding, and seeing patterns in symbols and shapes.

Whiz Kid

Bill Gates

William (Bill) H. Gates III was born on 28 October, 1955, and was programming computers at age 13, a sure sign of logical intelligence. At Harvard University, he developed a version of the programming language BASIC, demonstrating his abstract reasoning abilities with codes. In his junior year, Gates dropped out of Harvard to devote his energies full-time to Microsoft, a company he had started in 1975. His creative thinking led him to believe that the personal computer would be a valuable tool on every office desktop and in every home, so he began developing software for them. Today, Microsoft is the world's leading provider of software for personal computers.

DEVELOPING THINKING SMART AT HOME

If your child goes to nursery or school, you may feel that he spends the whole day thinking. However, the emphasis in schools is very much on logical thought, so you really can help your child by introducing him to the other types of thinking. Also, your child may not be aware that he is using logic to learn at school, so it is important to introduce the concept. The valuable skill of using logic to answer questions and solve problems will be the root of your child's learning.

You can introduce creative thinking as an early stage in logical thought. Encourage your child to spend time

thinking creatively around a problem before he commits to an answer. That way your child will come up with the best possible solution.

HELPING YOUR CHILD WITH THE ACTIVITIES

The thinking-smart assessments have been designed to be fun, and to demonstrate the different thinking styles. Cognitive development is very much age related, and true logical thinking doesn't really show itself until the age of seven.

Don't try to use all the thinking smart tests in one session. Your child may be quite tired after each one because the tests require real concentration. The logical thinking exercise will seem like a school test to your child, so only undertake it if he is in the right frame of mind. The abstract thinking and creative thinking

exercises will seem much more like games, and can be great for when he is bored or you have an hour to fill.

WHAT TO LOOK FOR

Younger children often find it difficult to use reasoning, since they may only just be starting to think logically. The creative thinking test will probably be the easiest to start with because a young child's fertile imagination can act as a springboard into this type of activity.

Always remember that your role is to help your child develop reasoning, so use the clues if you need to, and be sure to focus on his understanding of the tasks rather than the eventual outcome. Present the tests as 'puzzles', rather than as assessments.

First lessons in logic

The discipline of using step-by-step reasoning in order to find the best possible solution to a problem or sort through information is a valuable life skill. Logical thinking will help your child resolve disputes, quickly pick up new subjects in school, and make sense of the outside world.

1 What's the pattern?

Sit down with your child and explain that she needs to look at the pictures carefully. Talk about the patterns you can see all around you, both visual (stripes on a T-shirt) and conceptual (apples and pears are both fruit). You may need to use the clues or point to the relevant part of the picture to keep your child's attention, but let her try first.

Clues
1. They're all animals, aren't they?
2. Sun, moon, sun, moon … what comes next?
3. This is like a sum … if you add a square and the circle, you get a circle in the square.
4. A rectangle has straight sides, hasn't it?

Correct answers
1. A; 2. A; 3. C; .4 B.

How did it go?
If your child got two or fewer answers correct, it is probably because she is only just learning about 'logic', and tends to be impulsive by nature! Encourage your child not to rush, and to talk through why she chose a particular answer. After the test, you can use the questions to teach her about recognising patterns and problem solving.

   If your child got three or more answers correct, she is well on the way to being a logical thinker. You could use the test questions as a template for writing your own logic problems and improve her grasp of logic even further.

Boosting activities
- Find some old magazines, and let your child browse through them. Decide on a category – for example things that are blue, or things that you can find at home – and cut out any pictures in that category. You could then make a collage by sticking the pictures on to a large sheet of paper.
- Children love to collect things, and it's a great hobby because it helps them learn to sort and classify information. If your child doesn't already have a collection, encourage her to start one, maybe of postcards, pebbles or a particular type of toy – something that fascinates her. Talk about the different ways you could categorise the items, such as by country, size or colour, and then help your child put the items into the different groups.

Creative thinking

Thinking creatively involves widening your options when solving a problem rather than narrowing them down. This free-thinking exercise will help your child to apply imaginative solutions to practical problems – a crucial factor for success in future life.

2 Brainstorming

The point of this exercise is to encourage your child to be as imaginative as possible. Brainstorming is useful for tackling a situation where unusual and new ideas, rather than obvious and boring ones, are needed. It is excellent for unlocking and loosening the thought processes. Young children generally need some prompting, so use the following suggestions to get your child started:

1. Animals...Toys...Bananas
2. Eat ice cream for breakfast...Not have a bath...Go camping.
3. A spider sat down beside me....It disappeared when I picked up my fork....The dog ate it....

How did it go?
Did your child
• Understand the activity?
• Enjoy coming up with ideas?
• Seem able to produce lots of suggestions?
• Really get into the spirit of the activity?
• Demonstrate an increased interest in creative thinking after the activity?
If the answer is "Yes" to three or more of these questions, then your child is clearly learning to use her brain with dexterity.

   If the answer is "No" to three or more of these questions, then your child may not yet realise that creativity can be harnessed consciously. Children use their imaginations all the time in play, so your child's ability to think creatively is just waiting to be discovered and developed!

Boosting activities
• Improve your child's ability to generate ideas by suggesting a subject and asking her to tell you about as many items or activities as possible that relate to it. For instance, you could ask your child about all the possible ways a person could travel to school, or to list all the places in the world that she could hide a favourite toy.
• An important element in creative thinking is the ability to see the world in different ways to how you normally perceive it. You can help your child appreciate that there are many different ways of living or values in life by teaching her about other communities and cultures. Visit your local 'Chinatown', or go out for a Thai, Indian or Italian meal. Talk about how different people live.

Abstract reasoning

This type of thinking involves seeing patterns in symbols and shapes and decoding them. It enables children to understand that familiar things can be represented in different ways, which is essential when learning how to play a musical instrument or to speak a new language.

3 Secret messages

Your child should write the letters of the alphabet or her name on a piece of paper, leaving space next to each letter. You can do this for a younger child. Ask your child to create a unique symbol next to each letter, and make a copy so that you both know which letter of the alphabet each symbol represents.

If you have a computer, you could use either Zapf Dingbats or Symbol fonts.

For example A=▮, B=✛, C=●, D=▲, E=▼, F=◗

How did it go?

Did your child
- Understand the activity?
- Come up with the right solution for Mollie?
- Create her own code?
- Enjoy writing secret messages?
- Become more interested in codes after the activity?

If the answer is 'Yes' to three or more of the above, then your child is demonstrating a great grasp of abstract concepts and the idea that codes can be created and interpreted by others.

If the answer is 'No' to three or more of these questions, then your child may find that thinking in abstract terms does not come naturally, and is probably more creatively minded. Try the boosting activities to encourage abstract reasoning in your child.

Boosting activities
- Learn some words of an unfamiliar language and use them together. You could buy or borrow a simple phrasebook or a language learning tape for the car. This activity reinforces the idea that something may be represented by a different word but still have the same meaning.
- Go on a treasure hunt! Make a map of your home or garden and use symbols to represent the objects in it. Mark the treasure (a small gift, or sweets) with an 'X' on the map. Give your child the map and see if she can interpret the symbols and find the treasure.

WHAT IS PICTURE SMART?

Can you imagine a cereal box? Now flip it round in your head so that you can see the top and back, and try to view it from different angles. That's the essence of picture smart – being able to see images and objects in your mind as clearly as if they were really in front of you! Being picture smart means you can read a map to find your way to an unfamiliar place, or take things apart and put them back together again with ease. You have a sense of objects and the space they inhabit.

The picture smart tasks look at four areas:
- **Spatial reasoning** – the ability to think through visual problems and come up with the answers.
- **2D activities** – the ability to visualise in two dimensions.
- **3D objects** – the ability to mentally manipulate objects in three dimensions.
- **Mazes** – the ability to orientate yourself in two dimensions to find a route through branching paths (a maze) or a single twisting and turning path (a labyrinth).

ENCOURAGING SPATIAL INTELLIGENCE AT HOME

Developing 'picture smartness' in your child involves getting him to focus on the visual side of things. It can be particularly relaxing for a child who spends much of his time at school learning through words to spend time in the visual world. Some children with dyslexia have been found to be very picture smart.

You can help your child become more visually aware by making sure your home is a learning environment and filled with the necessary artistic materials (*see pages 10–14*) in order to stimulate his imagination. Turn off the TV and spend time together creating a picture or a model. Let your child take the lead.

Whiz Kid

Pablo Picasso

The son of an academic painter, Pablo Picasso was born in 1881 in Malaga, Spain. He began to draw at an early age and at the age of eight, produced his first oil painting 'The Picador''. In 1895, he moved with his family to Barcelona and studied at La Lonja, the academy of fine arts. His first exhibition took place in 1900. Picasso's 'picture smart' abilties encompassed at least three dimensions: he also collaborated on ballet and theatrical productions and he was a proficient sculptor. He produced a prolific amount of work including paintings, drawings, prints, ceramics and sculpture.

The first task, changing shapes, looks at spatial reasoning. It has a format similar to school tests, so don't attempt it if your child is tired. The 'Smart art' and 'Do it in 3D!' tests are art projects and are really fun, when you have sufficient time.

The final test involves mazes and labyrinths, which children seem to love, and there are lots of ideas for extending the maze theme.

WHAT TO LOOK FOR

Younger children particularly will enjoy the art activities but they may find the spatial reasoning tests difficult. Picture smart is quite conceptual, so it may be difficult for younger children to understand some of the activities.

If your child complains that he can't draw, or isn't good at ar, build up his confidence – everyone is picture smart in at least one way, you just need to find it.

Focus on the visual and spatial element of the activities. You shouldn't be too concerned about the neatness of drawing or the mess that may ensue with making things. Ask yourself whether your child seems to have a clear vision of what he is setting out to achieve.

HELPING YOUR CHILD WITH THE ACTIVITIES

Do explain to your child what picture smart means. You should focus on two dimensions if your child is young and introduce three dimensions when he is sufficiently old to grasp the concept. Use the analogy of the cereal box; ask your child to 'flip' it round in his head so he can see the top and back and view it from different angles – to explain the sort of thinking the tests will explore.

Talk about how picture smart is used in everyday life, for instance in assembling a new toy, or reading a map, as well as the sort of work people do who are picture smart. Architects, designers, engineers, artists and builders all use different aspects of picture smart to create things.

Spatial reasoning

In the same way as we use reasoning to think through problems in thinking smart, we can reason with shapes and space, which is known as spatial reasoning. This is the ability to imagine shapes in our mind, and how they can be moved or transformed. Shapes can be in two or three dimensions, but it is generally harder to manipulate images in 3D.

4 Changing shapes

Explain to your child that he needs to look at the pictures carefully. Talk about how shapes can look like different things if they are seen from different angles – for instance, a banana can look like a bridge if it's on its side, or like a crescent moon if you hold it upright. Read through the instructions together, and make sure he understands the questions; you may need to point to the relevant part of the picture to keep his attention, or to use the clues.

Clues
1. The letter might be back-to-front.
2. The shape will be exactly the same in the picture.
3. Imagine turning the shapes around in your head.
4. The triangles might be different sizes.
5. Imagine if you pressed the sides together.

Correct answers
1. E; 2. C; 3. A; 4. 3; 5. A.

How did it go?
Three or more correct answers show that your child is showing a gift for spatial reasoning, and probably enjoys playing games with a strong visual element. Encourage him to maximise this ability by using visual aids when learning.

Two or fewer correct answers indicate that your child is yet to gain an awareness of perspective, which comes with life experience. Everyone is picture smart in some way, so your child's strengths may lie in the creative arts – or he may be a budding inventor!

Boosting activities
• Play games together that have a visual element in 2- or 3D, like tic-tac-toe, checkers or chess. These games help develop thinking smart as well as picture smart.
• Make your own jigsaw puzzles by sticking an image your child likes, such as a pop star or cartoon character, on to a backing card, and then cutting out random shapes. You could do this activity together and make each other puzzles to try to solve.

Visualising in two dimensions

Some people, such as artists, graphic designers, illustrators and photographers, have a specific talent for creating and manipulating two-dimensional, flat images. Children with this talent are drawn to visual stimuli. Many make better sense of information by drawing an ideas map while others may enjoy making cartoons, sketches or watercolours. Others get pleasure from looking at art and love trips to galleries and museums.

5 Smart art

Creating pictures with paper and art materials is something most children enjoy. Explain the tasks to your child and let him decide which one to create. Focus on his visual interpretation of each task rather than his skill or neatness.

Patterns in nature: You will need a tray or large flat surface on which your child can present his collection.

Face painting: You will need face paints, brushes, scrap paper, a pencil and a mirror.

Seeing things differently: You will need a magnifying glass and binoculars or a telescope.

How did it go?
Did your child
- Understand the activity?
- Enjoy presenting what he saw?
- Seem able to creatively interpret what he saw?
- Get into the spirit of the activity?
- Demonstrate an increased interest in pictures, photographs or art after the exercise?

If the answer is 'Yes' to three or more of these questions, then your child is definitely picture smart, and is able to express himself well in two dimensions. Try the next test, 'Do it in 3D!', to see if he has a flair for that, too.

If the answer is 'No' to three or more of these questions, it could be because these tests are on the creative side, and your child might be picture smart in terms of appreciation rather than creativity. Learn about famous paintings together, or try making a collage from recycled materials.

Boosting activities
- Give your child a notebook for doodling in. Doodling promotes important subconscious thinking, and he may get new ideas or inspiration from looking back at previous drawings and sketches.
- Have a picture conversation. Ask your child a question like 'What shall we have for dinner?' or 'What shall we do today?' Your child then draws his response (say, a pizza). You then draw something in return (like a piece of pepperoni, a tomato, or some mushrooms) to find out what toppings he would like, and so on.

Working in three dimensions

One of the key elements of picture smart is the ability to think about space – both objects in space and the space around you. This type of thinking calls on the ability to imagine three-dimensional objects in your head, and then to move around them in your mind and 'see' them from different angles. Children who can do this may not be aware that they have this ability, and not all picture-smart people are able to think in three dimensions.

6 Do it in 3D!

Most children are very territorial about their bedrooms, so here's a chance for your child to express his individuality through his, and get picture smart at the same time. Choose one or both of these projects for or with your child – 'Mobile magic' may be more appropriate for younger children, while 'Bedroom remix' is better for older children. You will need to supervise your child for safety reasons, but try not to intervene in the creative process. Focus on the 3D element of each task rather than the appearance or suitability of the outcome!

Mobile magic: You will need paper and pencil, wire hangers, pliers and thread and your child's cutouts or his selection of objects.

Bedroom remix: You will need some graph paper, a pencil, a tape measure, a ruler and scissors.

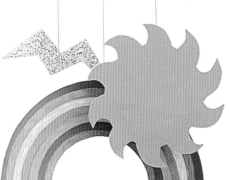

How did it go?
Did your child
- Understand the activity?
- Enjoy coming up with ideas and plans?
- Seem able to imagine the outcome in 3D?
- Really get into the spirit of the activity?
- Demonstrate an increased interest in space and three-dimensional images after the activity?

If the answer is 'Yes' to three or more of these questions, then your child has a talent for thinking in three dimensions, which is a special kind of picture smart. Encourage him to switch between 2D and 3D by drawing a 2D plan before he embarks on a 3D project.

If the answer is 'No' to three or more of these questions, your child is probably insufficiently mature, or he may be more comfortable working in two dimensions. Three-dimensional thinking tends to be something you either can or can't do, and lots of us find it difficult!

Boosting activities
- Make a papier-mâché head with your child by building up layers of newspaper strips dipped in a glue solution on to an inflated balloon. Leave the paper to dry, then decorate the 'head' by painting on a face and adding yarn for hair.
- Help your child to take apart an old tissue box carefully until it's a flat piece of cardboard. Then see if he can remake it using adhesive tape or glue. Seeing something in 3D, then 2D, then back to 3D again really demonstrates what picture smart is all about.

Labyrinths and mazes

Picture smart is about thinking in pictures and imagining objects in space. A fun way to explore this is to solve mazes. Mazes are puzzles made out of paths. They have a single destination but a number of dead ends in which you can get stuck. The oldest form of maze is the labyrinth, which has only one path and a central destination.

7 Amazing mazes

Sit down with your child and the mazes – you could photocopy the card if you don't want your child to write on it. Emphasise the basic rule of mazes – you have to enter where the arrow shows you and find your way out or to the centre without crossing a line.

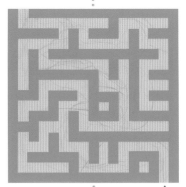

How did it go?
Did your child
- Understand the activity?
- Enjoy trying to reach the end or centre of the maze?
- Seem able to follow the right path with ease?
- Get into the spirit of the activity?
- Demonstrate an increased interest in mazes or labyrinths after the activity?

If the answer is 'Yes' to three or more of these questions, then your child is skillfully combining 2D picture smart with elements of thinking smart, as he mentally anticipates dead ends. The ability to plan ahead and predict problems before they actually arise is valuable in adult life.

If the answer is 'No' to three or more of these questions, it may be because your child is insufficiently mature, or he may prefer not to work in two dimensions. Some picture-smart people actually prefer working in 3D because it is more lifelike, so try some 3D activities together, like modelling or sculpting.

Boosting activities
- Pay a visit to a maze. Walking around a maze is a completely different experience to solving one on paper. Mazes can be made of hedges, brick walls and mirrors.
- Get your child to design his own maze, using a sheet of graph or grid paper. Trace a 30.5 x 30.5 cm (12 x 12 in) box, use a pencil to sketch the route and the 'dead ends', add the 'walls' in pen, and then erase the pencil lines. If this activity really arouses an interest in mazes, check out the internet for web sites with online mazes and labyrinths.

WHAT IS WORD SMART?

Formally known as linguistic intelligence, word smart refers to the ability to communicate with and understand both written and spoken words. It breaks down into three components – communication, self-expression and word-power. Children who can use words easily and gracefully in written or verbal form have a great head start for adult life. After all, verbal communication is the main method of human interaction. You can help your child to become word smart by encouraging him to use spoken language in a variety of ways and for different purposes.

Studies suggest that children who are advanced in language development come from homes where they encounter a rich variety of spoken and written language. In an attempt to introduce a passion for language into your home, surround your child with lots of printed material like storybooks, posters and magazines. Be a good role model and show him what you like to read and why you enjoy it. Strive for greater interaction with your child when reading stories out loud. Choose a relatively short tale that will hold his undivided attention. Stop and ask your child questions at key points. Using more 'why' rather than 'what' questions is a good way of teaching a child effective ways of self-expression and clear communication.

It is important for children to have someone to talk to in order to gain mastery over language, especially in the early years. Make sure that you and your child actively interact during any conversations that you have. Point out objects and people in your immediate environment, and discuss and categorise them.

HELPING YOUR CHILD WITH THE ACTIVITIES

When your child does the tests in this section, she will need a hands-on approach

Whiz Kid

Oprah Winfrey
Born on 29 January 1954, in Kosciusko, Mississippi into a small local farming community, Oprah Winfrey's grandmother taught her how to read and nourished her love of public speaking. By the age of three, she was reading the Bible and reciting in church. Winfrey's career as a television talkshow host, actress and producer had already begun.

and a lot of encouragement. Bear in mind that the majority of children love to talk, so what you as a parent are effectively evaluating is the manner and the diversity with which your child actually uses words, phrases, sentences and expressions, not her general level of talkativeness.

WHAT TO LOOK FOR

Your child will be more successful at carrying out the instructions so long as all that is required is the use of familiar vocabulary and a straightforward, factual style of verbal delivery. Take care to give your child lots of praise – after it's been earned, of course – to build up confidence and reward her effort and enthusiasm. Words of encouragement nourish verbal communication skills.

A child's love of language or talent for verbal communication will be evident in his speech through the confident use of humour, a wide and varied vocabulary range, or verbal details that are put forward in memorable ways to really engage an audience.

Spelling it out

Words, and the letters they contain, are the basic units of language, and word power is the ability to manipulate them confidently. If your child understands the different sounds each letter makes, the rules of sentence construction and is confident in using words, then she will find more complicated linguistic skills easier to acquire.

8 Letters and sounds

Sit down together, read through the instructions, and make sure your child understands the questions. She can respond verbally to you, or write the answers down, in which case you should have some paper and a pencil handy.

Clues
1. Look at the picture!
2. What are those pictures of?
3. Try saying these words aloud. Which ones sound the same?
4. What's a ... ? (Say each word in turn).
5. This is just like maths, but with letters instead of numbers.

Correct answers
1(A). My coat is green; (B). A dog can run.
2 (A). u; (B). o.
3 (A). D; (B). C.
4. A and C
5 (A). down; (B). fall.

How did it go?
If your child got five or fewer correct answers, she may only just be starting to learn about letters, their sounds, and how they make words. The key thing is to make words fun, so make up silly rhymes together, including as many quirky words as possible.

   If your child got six or more correct answers, she is demonstrating real word power potential, and probably enjoys reading. If she responded verbally, encourage her to write answers so she becomes more familiar with the written language.

Boosting activities
• Take the letter tiles from a Scrabble set, making sure you have lots of vowels and common consonants (b, c, d, g, l, m, p, s, t). Put the letters in a small, non-transparent bag and let your child pull out three or four. Arrange them on a table, talk about their names and sounds, and see if she can make any words out of them – real or nonsense ones.
• Children often feel real ownership of their names and the letters in them, so, using the letters in your child's name, go out somewhere together and see how many times she can spot the letters.

First steps in writing

You probably can't remember a time when you couldn't write, and it's difficult to appreciate the joy a child feels on finally being able to make a meaningful mark on a page that others can read. Younger children will need help so that they feel they are writing autonomously, even if they are just tracing letters or writing simple words.

9 All about me!

Help your child collect visual information to illustrate her life. This could be new or existing photos, old tickets for journeys or events, or pictures from magazines. Make sure the pictures cover a range of categories, such as family, holidays, hobbies or friends. Help your child paste the items in the scrapbook, grouping them as she wants, and leaving space around each one for a caption. Encourage your child to write as full a caption as possible by the appropriate picture. If necessary, your child can trace her captions over your writing, or dictate the caption to you. As well as being a valuable exercise, the scrapbook will make a lovely memento.

How did it go?
Did your child
- Understand the activity?
- Enjoy coming up with categories and pictures to illustrate her life?
- Find it easy to produce captions?
- Really get into the spirit of making the scrapbook?
- Demonstrate an increased interest in writing after the activity?

If the answer is 'Yes' to three or more of these questions, your child's language skills are well developed, and she is showing an aptitude for written language. This will become increasingly important when she starts school.

   If the answer is 'No' to three or more of these questions, your child is still developing her linguistic ability. Word-smart skills increase rapidly; you'll be surprised at how much progress your child can make in a very short time – there's a big difference in what a four-year-old and a six-year-old can achieve.

Boosting activities
- Help your child create her own library. Have her choose ten favourite books and help her write the title and author of each one on a separate index card and stick the appropriate card to the inside of the book. Keep all the books in a box, and when your child wants to borrow a book, she can stamp the card using a small 'stamper' (available from stationery shops). You can take it in turns to be the librarian and the reader and you could reinforce this activity with a trip to your local library.
- Include your child when you draw up your shopping list. She could trace over your writing, or you could help with spelling.

The spoken word

While children often mispronounce a word or make the odd grammatical mistake, being 'word smart' verbally has more to do with fluency and confidence with words. When learning a language, the only way to improve is to speak it as often as you can, in the presence of a someone who can correct you. As a parent, you should always encourage your child to try to articulate things, even if she is unsure of finding the right words or expressions.

10 Try a talking game

These are three word games that your child can play with you, and/or a sibling or a friend; the first two also are good when you are travelling or waiting somewhere. Play the following variations with a young child:

Under my bed: the players don't have to remember the previous items, just make up something new each time.

Cooperation story: you can create the plot, leaving your child to add a few words rather than a whole sentence.

Watch your back!: you can let the child pick a picture and describe it to you without saying the name of it.

How did it go?
Did your child
- Understand the activity?
- Enjoy playing the games?
- Seem able to speak with ease?
- Really get into the spirit of the activity?
- Demonstrate an increased vocabulary or enthusiasm for speaking aloud after the activity?

If the answer is 'Yes' to three or more of these questions, then your child has a strong grasp of verbal language, and you probably talk a lot together as a family. She is likely to enjoy using words and language, and can express herself well.

If the answer is 'No' to three or more of these questions, then it could mean that your child found the games difficult to understand. Try easier variations to build her confidence.

Boosting activities
- Make time to have a proper conversation with your child every day. Use open questions, such as, 'What do you think we should do at the weekend?' or 'What would be your ideal meal?' Try to avoid an interrogative question about what happened at school!
- Encourage your child to speak with people you meet so that she becomes used to communicating with others who may have a strong accent or use unfamiliar words. It is a good way of expanding your child's vocabulary as well as boosting her social skills.
- Other popular games, such as 'I Spy' or '20 Questions' are great ways of passing the time constructively in the car, during intervals, or whenever you have spare time together.

WHAT IS NUMBER SMART?

Also known as numerical intelligence, this is the ability to use numbers confidently and successfully. Basic arithmetic is fundamental to number smart, but other key attributes are important too – such as the ability to reason and solve problems.

Whiz Kid

Srinivasa Aiyangar Ramunujan

Born in Southern India in 1887, Srinivasa was a great mathematical genius. All through his life, he was fascinated by numbers. At an early age, he studied trigonometry and pure mathematics on his own. He astounded his teachers with mathematical feats such as multiplying large numbers in his head. He later attended the Universities of Madras and then Cambridge, where he was elected fellow of Trinity College. Unfortunately his health was not good. He died aged 32, leaving behind his famous notebooks, through which modern mathematicians are still wading, trying to prove some of his theorems.

Number-smart children question, investigate and explore solutions to problems; demonstrate the ability to stick with a problem to find a solution; consider many different answers to a problem, and apply maths successfully to everyday situations, which is when it really comes alive for them. They also can use words, numbers or mathematical symbols to explain situations; to talk about how they arrived at an answer, and to listen to other people's ways of thinking, and, in addition to giving solutions to examples, they understand how maths works.

ENCOURAGING NUMERICAL INTELLIGENCE AT HOME

The most supportive thing you can do is to have a positive attitude to maths yourself. Since mathematics has become increasingly important in many modern technology-based careers, it is vital that children learn maths at home as well as at school. Involve your children in family decisions that use maths. Dividing up a pizza at mealtimes, counting change for a parking meter, or working out how much time your child can spend at a friend's house are all useful activities your child can participate in.

Learning maths is a process of solving problems and applying what has been learned to new questions. In today's schools, the focus is on understanding the concepts and applying thinking skills to arrive at an answer.

HELPING YOUR CHILD WITH THE ACTIVITIES

The number-smart tests have been designed to be fun, and to promote mathematical interaction between you and your child. The acquisition of maths is age-related, so these tests are suitable for children aged four to six years.

The first two tests assess basic arithmetic, and will give you an indication of the learning stage your child has reached. Bear this in mind when you tackle the following test, which looks at numerical reasoning – the use of maths in everyday life. Allow your child to work at her own pace, to take ownership of the activity and to enjoy it!

WHAT TO LOOK FOR

Young children generally will be enthusiastic about the activities. The essence of numerical intelligence is feeling comfortable around numbers and taking pleasure in problem-solving using numbers. You should, therefore, focus on exuberance rather than any error – it is your child's enthusiasm that will pay dividends in the years ahead.

You should watch out for any loss of confidence with maths and address it immediately with lots of support and practice. Number-smart children have a strong self-belief in their ability to use numbers successfully, and this is developed by being stretched, learning from mistakes, and perseverance.

First steps in mental arithmetic

The foundation to good maths skills is mental arithmetic, and kids aged four to six years should be able to add and subtract numbers under ten with confidence. Children need to be able to add and subtract all the time in their daily lives, for example when keeping score in a rugby game, or when saving money for a special treat.

11 Party animals

Sit down with your child and ask her to look at the picture carefully. The theme of this card is parties, so you could talk about a birthday party she recently has been to. Read through the instructions together, and make sure your child understands the questions. You may need to point to the relevant part of the picture to keep her focused.

Correct answers
1. Rabbit; 2. 12; 3. 7; 4. 6; 5. 6.

How did it go?
If your child got two or fewer answers correct, then she is just learning that numbers correspond to amounts of objects. Children first learn to count by rote (much as they learn a nursery rhyme by heart), but, by around the age of five, they gradually come to learn the significance of the numbers they are reciting. Encourage careful finger-pointing to actual objects when adding, and physically take away objects when subtracting.

If your child got three or more answers correct, it reveals she has reached a crucial stage in maths, and now understands numbers in a more abstract way – that is, she will know that 2+2=4 without needing to have four objects in front of her.

Boosting activities
• Buy some multi-coloured sweets, such as jelly beans or M&Ms. Ask your child to sort the sweets into groups of different colours, to estimate which pile has the most beans, and finally to count them to make sure. Sorting, estimating and counting are all key maths skills. You can extend this activity by rearranging the sweets and asking your child to re-count – many children will realise that the numbers remain the same. Finally, you could do some subtraction by eating the sweets!

• Make up 11 cards, with the numbers 0 to 10 on them, plus three others for '+', '-', and '='. See how many different sums both you and your child can create by rearranging the cards. You can vary this activity to make it as easy or as difficult for her as you like.

Using maths in real life

Shopping is a great way to get your child to appreciate the importance of maths in real life – and to have fun with it. Budgeting, planning what to buy, counting money and checking change are all key maths skills.

12 Candy and counting

Set out a selection of sweets, each group with a price per item, and give your child some coins of all denominations. Read through the questions on the card with your child and then let her 'buy' what she likes. Offer to help with adding or subtracting. Let your child enjoy the sweets and any leftover change!

How did it go?
Did your child
- Understand the activity?
- Enjoy using maths in a 'real life' situation?
- Show confidence when using numbers?
- Really get into the spirit of the 'shopping' trip?
- Demonstrate an increased interest in numbers after the activity?

If the answer is 'Yes' to three or more of these questions, then your child showed real number-smart potential.

If the answer is 'No' to three or more of these questions, your child needs some help in becoming number smart. Try to find out what she didn't like about the activity and see if you can modify it.

Boosting activities
- Ask for a clean chips container from your child's favourite fast-food chain. Take several yellow kitchen sponges and cut them into long strips – these will be the 'chips'. Set up a table as the counter: your child will be the employee, while you will play the customer. Ask your child for a certain number of chips and have her count them out. You could change your mind to let her practice subtraction.
- Ask your child to trace er shoe on to a piece of paper and use it to measure distances around your home. Use it to find out how many steps it takes to get from one place to another. How far is it from his bed to the bathroom, or from the sink to the kitchen table?

Numbers in everyday life

Numbers are used in lots of different ways to provide us with essential information in everyday life – think of how hard it would be to find a house without its number or to buy new clothes without a price tag to guide you. The purpose of this activity is to help your child discover the significance and meaning of numbers in daily life.

13 Number hunt!

Explore your house or neighbourhood with your child and encourage her to write down all the places numbers are found and what they mean. The examples shown on the card include a bar code, washing machine dial, clock radio, thermometer, ruler, calculator and clock. Outdoor examples could include buses or house numbers.

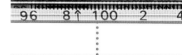

How did it go?
Did your child
- Understand the activity?
- Enjoy finding the numbers?
- Show confidence in interpreting numbers and numerical values?
- Really get into the spirit of finding numbers in everyday life?
- Demonstrate an increased interest in numbers after the activity?

If the answer is 'Yes' to three or more of these questions, then your child is showing real number-smart potential. Try extending this activity by presenting the findings in a table. Creating and understanding tabular numerical information is a great maths skill, and important for reading school or travel timetables.

If the answer is 'No' to three or more of these questions, then your child may need more encouragement to develop her numerical skills. Talk about numbers whenever you can: those on a remote control or on sports shirts, or in addresses and telephone numbers. Ask your child why we use numbers in these situations.

Boosting activities
- Keep a record of your child's height and weight. Let her read the scales and measure the height mark, and note it down in a special place. You even could draw a graph over time to show how she has grown.
- Estimating is an important everyday skill and an excellent back-up when using calculators – we've all forgotten to add a number, or slipped a finger on the number pad. Ask your child to guess the number of sweets in a jar, the value of coins in your wallet, or the heaviest toy in her room.

WHAT IS BODY SMART?

How you use your body – your control of it and your ability to use it skillfully in combination with other objects – is what's known as body smart. We often find it difficult to think of our bodies as 'intelligent' because although we perform a vast and varied amount of tasks throughout the day, most are at a sub-conscious level. But our bodies don't just do their own thing as we walk, drive or reach for a product on a supermarket shelf. Our minds are coordinating all the movement.

Think about a world-class athlete running a marathon. She will have formulated a strategy for the race. She calculates speed as she runs, and knows when to slow down to avoid burnout. She is coordinating her muscles and breathing, and she has the physical fitness to run for hours. So a lot of brain power is involved! But body smart is not only about sport; other body-smart people include dancers, actors, painters and even dentists.

The tests in this chapter look at four main aspects of body smart:

- **Hand-eye coordination** – the ability to use the hands precisely to control objects.
- **Whole-body coordination** – the ability to coordinate the entire body's movements.
- **Balance** – the ability to maintain and manage movement despite changes in environment.
- **Flexibility** – the ability to undertake a wide variety of movement through the suppleness of the joints.

ENCOURAGING PHYSICAL INTELLIGENCE AT HOME

Not all of us will be brilliant athletes, or have the potential to earn a living as a performing artist, but we all need to be healthy, have strong muscles and joints and to avoid strain injuries in later life.

Whiz Kid

Venus and Serena Williams

The Williams sisters grew up in Los Angeles and both started playing tennis when they were just four years old, using old balls that they found. They were coached by their father, who taught himself to play from a book.

When Venus was nine and Serena was eight, they entered their first tennis tournament. Both girls reached the final and Venus beat her younger sister. Venus turned professional when she was 14, and quickly climbed the world ranking followed by her sister. The two made tennis history in 2001, when they became the first African-American sisters to play each other in a US Open final.

HELPING YOUR CHILD WITH THE ACTIVITIES

The body-smart tasks are designed to give you an impression of your child's strengths and preferences: either whole-body control, part-body control, or the careful manipulation of objects. The activities also should be enjoyable, and will appeal to children regardless of their physical ability.

Give plenty of praise and try doing some of the activities yourself. Not only will you set a great example but children love seeing their parents make fools of themselves! Remember that you are trying to instil a lifelong interest in physical activity and body skills, so focus on having fun rather than criticising performance. Body smart is one of those intelligences a child easily can improve – it just takes practice.

WHAT TO LOOK FOR

Young children are likely to be clumsy because their coordination of brain and body isn't yet fully mature. Your child is more likely to do well on the flexibility tasks than the balance or whole-body coordination ones. Children aged four to six can have very good hand-eye coordination, but any craft activities will still be a bit messy!

Look for signs that your child is particularly relishing an activity or an aspect of a task, as this is the best indicator of future promise. A child who enjoys something is more likely to practise it, and thus improve.

Many of us have hobbies that involve using our hands, or get enjoyment from expressing ourselves artistically. These are pleasures we can pass on to our children.

As with many 'smarts', the best thing you can do is to set a good example yourself and be active with your family. Sporty parents tend to naturally encourage their children to try out different activities, but if you aren't this way inclined, you need to make an effort to add physical activity to your routine. Go on a picnic in the park and play ball games. Or do something creative together – model a clay bowl and paint it, or make necklaces and bracelets from beads and string. Get active and get creative!

Hand-eye coordination

The following activities can determine how well your child is able to use his hands together with his eyes in order to accomplish a given task accurately. Your child will use this skill, for example, when learning to write, while playing tennis or reaching for a glass of milk.

14 Cut, stick and construct

Choose one or all of these projects for or with your child. If necessary, allow your child some practice time before observing and evaluating his hand-eye coordination. Focus on the synchronicity between hand and eye, rather than creative flair or sheer strength.

Make a model: Give your child some newspaper and cardboard, glue, adhesive tape and scissors. Have paints on hand to make the model look more realistic.

Paint a picture: Give your child paper and paints or colouring pens, pencils or crayons. Observe his skill in adding fine detail (like buttons on clothing or eyebrows), pointing out such details, if necessary.

Construct a collage: Offer your child a variety of dried beans, peas, and pasta and some glue, along with paper on which to form a picture.

How did it go?

Your child should have been able to use materials or handle objects with some dexterity, although the outcome won't be precise or even particularly tidy. Look out for your child's care and concentration during the task. Kinesthetic intelligence can be developed and refined throughout life, so having the opportunity to practice it while having fun is the most important thing!

Boosting activities

- Cut two lengths of string about 60 cm (2 feet) long. Twist one into any shape – it can be a random or a recognisable image. Get your child to replicate your design using his own piece of string. Take it in turns being the copier.
- Place a scatter cushion on the floor about 1.5 m (5 feet) away from you. Have your child throw a beanbag (or a soft toy) at the cushion so that the beanbag (or toy) lands on or touches it.

Whole-body coordination

This is to do with how well you can use your mind to control your body – either one part, like using your hands to play a guitar, or your entire body, for when you run, climb or play football. And it's not just musicians or sports people who can use their whole bodies in clever ways; if your child shows good whole-body coordination potential, he might become a dancer or perform stunts.

15 Move your body

This is a good way of encouraging your child to use his whole body for self-expression, and to think about how he should move to convey information. Your child will mime four things: a dog, drummer, kangaroo, and fisherman. You are looking for whole-body coordination, rather than accurate acting skills, so make sure that – eventually – you guess correctly.

How did it go?
Did your child
- Understand the activity?
- Enjoy miming?
- Seem able to move with ease?
- Really get into the spirit of the activity?
- Demonstrate an increased interest in whole-body movement after the test?

If the answer is 'Yes' to three or more of these questions, it indicates your child is at ease with his body and able to control it well – a sure sign of being body smart. He probably enjoys sport, too.

If the answer is 'No' to three or more of these questions, remember that whole-body coordination is just one area of body smart. Your child's strengths may lie in using individual body parts such as his hands. Or, it may have been that the expressive nature of this task was inhibiting to him.

Boosting activities
- Make time to exercise together as a family – go hiking, ride bikes, or swim regularly at your local pool. You could even have a family 'disco' night, where you get dressed up, turn the lights down and dance around your living room to music. Get your child to work out a dance routine that you all learn and follow!
- Play 'Blind Penny Hunt', which works best with more than one player. Clear an open space in a room, removing any dangerous objects, and scatter pennies on the floor. Blindfold the children and give each one a paper bag. The players then crawl around the floor, feeling for pennies and collecting any they find in their bags. After five minutes, remove the blindfolds and check each bag – the winner is the child with the most pennies.

Flexibility

This refers to the amount of movement you have around your joints. Babies and children are extremely flexible, but muscle elasticity gradually decreases with age. Maintaining flexibility in children sets them on the path of healthy and safe joint movement, which is crucial for preventing injury in later life.

16 Yoga zoo

Having muscle and joint flexibility is recognised as being both physically and medically beneficial.This exercise uses yoga poses that kids will find enjoyable to perform. Yoga aims to connect the body and the mind by teaching you to be aware of your body as you move it into the different postures. This mental element makes it a great technique for developing 'body smartness'.

Practise these positions together, being careful not to push your child into any of the postures. Encourage your child to 'listen' to her body and to stop when she has had enough.

How did it go?
Did your child
- Understand the activity?
- Enjoy forming the postures with you?
- Seem able to get into the postures with ease?
- Really get into the spirit of yoga?
- Demonstrate an increased interest in yoga or flexibility after the activity?

If the answer is 'Yes' to three or more of these questions it shows your child has great flexibility. Your child's healthy joints will be a great asset as he matures. Make sure you incorporate flexibility activities into your child's everyday life to keep his joints supple.

If the answer is 'No' to three or more of these questions, it could be because your child had difficulty understanding the task, rather than with his flexibility. If your child can move easily, sit cross-legged, turn his body at the waist, or touch his toes, then he is displaying flexibility.

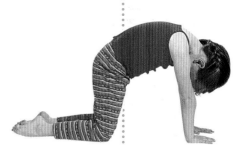

Boosting activities
- Write the name of ten different body parts (e.g. 'arm', 'elbow', 'hand', 'leg', 'knee', 'foot', 'stomach', 'head', 'ankle', and 'bottom') on small pieces of paper, and put them in a bag. Ask your child to pick two pieces of paper from the bag at random and then try to make those parts of the body touch each other. Play together and you'll have a hilarious time trying to achieve some of the combinations!
- Try limbo dancing. Position or hold a broom or mop handle horizontally so that your child has to bend backwards from the waist to move under the pole without touching it or losing his balance. Start at nose height, and gradually lower the pole. Add some steel drum music for extra fun!

Balance

This is the ability to assume and maintain a position or activity, and to adjust your centre of gravity to match your movement. It is much harder to remain steady while moving, yet our brains adjust to these changes automatically as we walk, jump or run. Shifting your centre of gravity on purpose is an important exercise in encouraging your brain and body to work together.

17 Balancing act

Choose any or all of the ideas listed below. If you do this activity indoors, make sure the surroundings are safe in case your child falls.

Circus tightrope: Place a skipping rope, or a length of string on the floor in a straight line. Your child has to walk the length of the rope without 'falling off'.

Sack race: Give your child an old pillowcase, and mark the starting and finishing lines. Your child stands in his pillowcase at the starting line, and has to jump all the way to the finishing line without falling over.

Pirate treasure: Fill a paper bag with small items such as coins, sweets or marbles. Have your child balance this 'treasure' on his head, and then escape from you back to the 'pirate ship' – this could be another room, up the stairs, or the end of the garden – without dropping the treasure.

Crossing the river: Lay out five large pieces of paper in a path as 'rocks' your child has to jump on. If your child touches the floor, he has fallen in the river.

How did it go?
Did your child
- Understand the activity?
- Enjoy the games?
- Seem able to maintain his balance while moving?
- Really get into the spirit of the activities?
- Demonstrate an increased awareness of balance after the test?

If the answer is 'Yes' to three or more of these questions, then your child has great balance and is very body smart. The ability to maintain a centre of gravity, even when the body moves or is carrying something, will help him stay healthy and reduce the chances of injury.

If the answer is 'No' to three or more of these questions, then your child probably found that balancing when moving or carrying a load takes a while to adjust to. Improving body balance is really a matter of practice, so encourage your child to have fun exploring it.

Boosting activities
- Get your child to help carry things for you, such as a light bag of groceries, or the dishes from the dining table, whenever possible. When we carry objects, our brain and body have to work together to adjust to the extra weight; this is great for developing body smart.
- Encourage your child to try a new sport that has a focus on balance. Together, you could go ice-skating, roller-blading, trampolining or take classes in a martial art like judo.

This is the ability to perceive, create and express music in all its forms. Musical intelligence develops very early, and a parent's voice or sung lullaby soothes even a tiny baby. Toddlers often make up tunes, and love exciting songs and ones with gestures.

Music smart can be 'top-down', as in having an empathic and intuitive appreciation of music, personified in someone who is uplifted and inspired by musical notes and beats. It also can be 'bottom-up', as in having an analytical and technical understanding of music, possessed by those who compose and perform music to high standards.

Making music calls on a number of other intelligences, too. Counting beats and learning about the structure of music depends on number- and thinking-smart skills, and you are coordinating your body in order to produce notes, using body-smart abilities. Music is a powerful method of communicating with others, literally and emotionally, so music smart can also help with people-smart skills.

TYPES OF MUSIC SMART

The tests in this chapter look at four main aspects of music smart:

- **Pitch** – the ability to detect sounds on a musical scale, from high to low notes.
- **Rhythm** – the ability to feel and produce the beat of music, used to measure time throughout a musical piece.
- **Listening to music** – the ability to appreciate and understand music.
- **Making music** – the ability to generate music using the voice or an instrument.

ENCOURAGING MUSICAL INTELLIGENCE AT HOME

Children love music and even pre-crawling babies will sit and 'bob' to a rhythm. Music is a safe environment for expressing feelings and emotions that are difficult for children to talk about, so it should be encouraged as an emotional outlet. A successful rendition of a song or musical piece gives children a wonderful sense of achievement and raised self-esteem. Playing or singing in a group helps children's social skills, as they mix with others outside of their established network of friends.

Whiz Kid

Wolfgang Amadeus Mozart

Born in Salzburg, Germany, in 1756, Wolfgang Amadeus Mozart was an exceptional music-smart prodigy. He played the violin at three, and composed at five. He made his first pubic appearance at age six, in a harpsichord and piano concert tour of Munich and Vienna. One year later (1763), his first published composition was distributed in Paris. Mozart became Konzertmeister (at age 13) to the Archbishop of Salzburg. He possessed perfect pitch, and at age 14, he heard Allegri's 'Miserere' at the Sistine Chapel and wrote down the score after one hearing. He produced a vast quantity of work but died at the age of 35.

HELPING YOUR CHILD WITH THE TESTS

The first two activities assess the main elements of music – pitch and rhythm. Having gauged your child's innate ability with these skills, you can have some fun listening to and making music in the next two tests.

A love of music is something we are all born with, but somewhere along the line we may tag ourselves with labels, such as 'no good at singing' or 'can't read music'. If your child seems to be wearing one of these tags, you will need to build up her confidence to shake it off. Start by introducing music as fun before you attempt any of the tests – children need to be enjoying themselves before they reveal their talents to you.

WHAT TO LOOK FOR

Young children are likely to enjoy all of the activities, but may have difficulty understanding the concepts of pitch and rhythm. Spend some time on pitch and rhythm if you feel your child would benefit from it.

A child with exceptional musical abilities will find the tests quite easy, and will really relish doing them. If music plays a major part in your child's life, if she makes up songs, hums while completing tasks or remembers melodies easily, the chances are she is music smart.

There are lots of ways you can encourage music smart at home, some need resources, others – such as singing – don't.

If your child has the opportunity to play an instrument at school, then encourage her to take it, and try to extend playing opportunities by finding out about local orchestras and bands she could take part in. If your child enjoys singing, she may be able to join a church or school choir.

Pitch

When a musical instrument is played it causes the air around it to vibrate. Our ears pick up these vibrations, and our brain interprets them as sound. If the vibration is steady, we hear it as a musical note. If it vibrates quickly, we hear a high note or pitch; if it vibrates slowly, we hear a low note or pitch. Recognising the differences in pitch is an important part of being music smart. Some people are 'tone deaf', in that they cannot reproduce or tell the difference between notes.

18 Pitch it right

You will need three drinking glasses, some water and a small spoon. Explain to your child that you are going to play a guessing game with musical notes. Your child should fill one glass with a small amount of water, the second so it is about half full, and the third glass so the water almost reaches the top. You may have to help small children. When your child is seated with her back to the glasses, strike the rim of one glass with your spoon to produce a target note. Then three seconds later, play another – either the same note, or one of the other glasses. Ask your child to tell you if the note was the same or different. Repeat until she has guessed whether five notes are the same or different.

How did it go?

Three or more correct answers reveal your child has excellent pitch, and is probably already demonstrating an affinity for music through singing or listening to music. Your child may go on to develop perfect pitch.

Two or fewer correct answers indicate that she has average pitch, and probably found it difficult to hear subtle differences between the notes. While pitch is an important aspect of music smart, there are lots of other ways to be musically intelligent.

Boosting activities

- Accompanied by your child, find five different water vessels around the house, and fill each with some water. You could choose a jug, a vase or even a bucket. Ask her to strike the rim of each one with a spoon, and then to arrange them in order of pitch, from the lowest to the highest. You can extend this activity by asking your child to try to sing the note that each vessel produces as it is struck.
- Play 'Name that Tune' together. Take turns to hum or guess a tune to a well-known nursery or folk song – try 'She'll be Coming Round the Mountain', 'Three Blind Mice', or 'Rudolph the Red-Nosed Reindeer'. If you have a piano or keyboard, you can do the same activity while playing the notes.

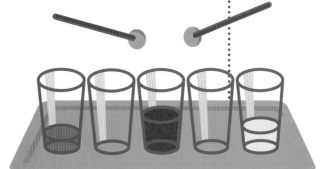

Rhythm and rhyme

Rhythm is the beat or pulse of a piece of music. If you find yourself swaying or tapping your feet to a song you love then your body is sensing and responding to its rhythm. Just as rhythm and pitch are the essence of music, so is a feeling for rhythm central to being music smart. Rhymes produce 'catchy' lyrics!

19 Keep to the beat!

Your child is going to write some new lyrics for the well-known nursery rhyme tune, 'Frère Jacques'. Ask her to chose words that reflect the rhythm of the tune, express an idea and rhyme at the end of the appropriate lines. Help your child listen for the syllables in words, as each syllable is a separate beat.

How did it go?
Did your child

- Understand the activity?
- Enjoy coming up with lyrics to reflect her interests or ideas?
- Understand the rhythm and rhymes of the tune?
- Really get into the spirit of the activity?
- Demonstrate an increased interest in rhythm and rhyme after the activity?

If the answer is 'Yes' to three or more of these questions, then your child's sense of rhythm is well developed, and she is likely to enjoy dancing and clapping to the beat. A great sense of rhythm means great music-smart ability!

If the answer is 'No' to three or more of these questions, then your child may not yet have discovered rhythm. You can encourage her by dancing or clapping along together to some music. Remember, rhythm can be very sociable!

Boosting activities
- Most classical Western music has very ordered and measured rhythm: the lengths of individual notes are exact multiples or subdivisions of each other. A lot of 'American' music has two separate rhythms, one for the drums and another for vocals. African music is known for its polyrhythms, which are many different rhythms that are played at the same time. Listen together to music from other cultures so you can pick out the different rhythms.
- Using your smart phone or other recorder, help your child capture everyday sounds with distinctive rhythms. Around your home you could listen to the sound of your washing machine or the phone ringing, and while you're outdoors, explore the sounds of birdsong, street repairs, or a train clattering across tracks.

Listening to music

Most music is written to express or invoke an emotion or feeling, and this is achieved through both the melody and the lyrics. Therefore, music smart has close links with self smart, and is a safe and personal vehicle for adults and children alike to consider thoughts and emotions. This exercise will help your child understand music's emotional aspects, as well as encouraging active listening to and enjoyment of music, both of which are important elements in being music smart.

20 Feel the music

Set aside some time, maybe at the end of the day, when your child is likely to sit quietly. Listen together in silence to two contrasting tracks of music – one happy and uplifting, the other sombre and sad. Then listen again, and afterwards talk about the emotions each track conveys.

How did it go?
Did your child
- Understand the activity?
- Enjoy listening to the music and talking about it with you?
- Seem able to describe the pieces accurately?
- Really get into the spirit of the activity?
- Demonstrate an increased interest in listening to music after the activity?

If the answer is 'Yes' to three or more of these questions, then your child is great at actively listening to music – a sure sign of music smart, and an ability that will give her great pleasure in adult life.

If the answer is 'No' to three or more of these questions it is probably because young children love music for music's sake, not particularly as a form of communication. Encourage this basic love, because a deeper appreciation of music will follow.

Boosting activities
- Expose your child to various kinds of music. Pick out a few examples of different genres of music from your own collection – jazz, pop, hip-hop, dance, classical, country, gospel, reggae or rock. Play some tracks to illustrate these music types and talk about what your child likes and doesn't like, and why.
- Take your child to hear live music. Watch musicians express themselves through singing or playing. There is often free live music at fairs, festivals, parks or local schools.

Making music

Singing or playing a musical instrument is probably the most evident way of being music smart, and these are the skills that come to mind when we think of musical intelligence. If your child already plays an instrument, or sings in the school choir, you'll know if she is 'musical' in some way. But children who sing along to the radio, or drum their hands on the table, are also showing their ability to make music.

21 Rubber-band violin

Gather together a tissue box, six rubber bands and a pencil, and sit together at a table. There should be no background noise. Once your child has made the violin and bow, see that she explores the sounds made with the bow and by plucking the 'strings'. Focus on the musical aspects of this activity rather than your child's craft skills.

How did it go?
Did your child
- Understand the activity?
- Enjoy making sounds with the violin and bow?
- Seem able to produce notes, or even a tune?
- Really get into the spirit of the activity?
- Demonstrate an increased interest in making music after the activity?

If the answer is 'Yes' to three or more of these questions, then your child's music-making abilities are a definite indication of music smart. You might want to develop this skill by taking her to a children's music group or paying for music tuition.

If the answer is 'No' to three or more of the these questions, then it could indicate your child may not have discovered music making for herself yet, or it could mean her music-smart talents simply lie in another direction.

Boosting activities
- Your child needs to hear music to be able to play or create it. Sing along to music in the car, or listen to it instead of watching the TV. Let your child choose the CD. Music is also thought to help stimulate thinking, concentration and memory.
- Try making other musical instruments such as a drum from a bucket or flower pot, a rattle from a plastic pot filled with beans, or a horn from blowing across the top of an empty bottle. You could have a 'jamming session' at home, with every member of your family playing together!

WHAT IS PEOPLE SMART?

This ability helps us understand other people and their moods, motivations and intentions. It enables us to tune in to others, to empathise with them, to communicate clearly with them emotionally, to inspire them and to understand our relationships with them.

Children who are people smart genuinely like others, and tend to have a wide variety of friendships. They might be good at resolving conflicts, or are natural leaders. They are good at 'reading' people, pick up emotional vibes easily and accurately, and reach out to those in need such as shy kids, or the less popular at school. In turn, they are easy people to be around, and sought after as play partners.

There are four people-smart tests; each covers one of the main skills in emotional intelligence:

- **Communication of emotions** – understanding how people use their voice and sometimes gestures when they feel different emotions.
- **Conflict resolution** – the ability to problem-solve and negotiate satisfactory solutions to relationship problems. Teaching problem-solving to children helps them to have happy, safe, and secure relationships.
- **Forming and sustaining friendships** – the ability to make new friends and enable existing friendships to thrive.
- **Coping with social setbacks** – the ability to remain optimistic in the face of social rejection, and to speculate positively on reasons for the setback.Parents who help their kids see that social situations can be improved with effort and positive behaviour, will raise them to have an optimistic view of others and themselves as friends.

ENCOURAGING EMOTIONAL INTELLIGENCE

Healthy friendships are a crucial part of childhood, and vital to your child's healthy development. Through friends, your child is learning how to get along with people, to understand his and others' emotions, to negotiate, cooperate and compromise. You can help your child by expanding his circle of friends: invite a new child to play, or encourage your child to join a club based on his interests. Teach your child to be assertive, to let others know that he wants to play, or that his feelings are hurt, or that he doesn't like it when another child pushes him.

Whiz Kid

Margaret Thatcher

Margaret Hilda Roberts was born in 1925 in Grantham, England. A clever child whose father was an ardent worker in local politics, she decided early in life to become a Member of Parliament. She studied chemistry at Oxford University, where she was the first woman president of the Oxford University Conservative Association. In 1959, she won a seat in Parliament. Analytical, articulate and ambitious, she soon become prominent among other politicians. In 1974 she became leader of the Conservative Party and then was elected prime minister – the first woman in Europe to achieve this.

Talk with your child about what makes a good friend. Does he see, through your life, that he can be friends with anyone he chooses?

HELPING YOUR CHILD WITH THE ACTIVITIES

These tests require interaction between you and your child, by their very nature. The tests have been designed to encourage an open discussion between you. There are no right or wrong answers. It's very important that you approach the tests calmly and neutrally, to encourage your child to talk openly about his feelings and friendships. Make sure your child is 'in the mood', and don't push for answers if your child has clearly had enough. Respect his privacy and try again another day.

It is possible that during a test, your child may choose to reveal something you weren't expecting. If anything he says worries you, discontinue the test, and use the opportunity to probe gently. Don't lose your cool; take time out to consider the best course of action.

WHAT TO LOOK FOR

Young children tend to have a number if friendships, which are transient in nature. They are also egocentric, and less likely to see events from another child's perspective. However, now is a perfect time to sow the seeds of how your child makes and develops friendships.

You should view the tests as an opportunity to discuss friendship, feelings and relationships. Boys tend to favour a group of friends, and interactions are more activity-based, like playing games or sport. Girls tend to have a close circle of friends, and perhaps one special friend, and interactions include talking about feelings.

Non-verbal communication

People-smart adults and children have a great understanding of how others are feeling, what they need or want and why they act the way they do. Key skills for understanding this are listening and observing. People give clues about how they really feel, or what they really want, in the way that they speak, and in their facial expressions and body movements. Someone with sensitivity will pick up on these.

22 Emotional voices

Your child is going to try to identify emotions – which could be happiness, sadness, or anger – by your voice and your facial expression. Pick a well-known nursery rhyme or poem your child is familiar with and say it aloud to him, portraying different feelings – perhaps first sadness, then happiness and finally anger. Ask your child to say what he thinks you are – happy, sad or angry.

How did it go?
Did your child:
• Understand the activity?
• Enjoy guessing the emotions?
• Seem able to identify an emotion by the way you used your voice?
• Really get into the spirit of the activity?
• Demonstrate an increased interest in how people can use their voices or body language to convey emotion?

If the answer is 'Yes' to three or more of these questions, it reveals your child can sense emotion in voice and expressions, both crucial elements in being people smart. He is probably at ease in social situations that involve meeting new people.

If the answer is 'No' to three or more of these questions, then your child may be new to the concept of emotion as an element of speech or body language. Explain to him how people shout and tense up when they are cross, or how a voice 'lilts and the person relaxes when she is happy.

Boosting activities
• Watch a drama or film together on TV, and talk about what the characters might be feeling by the way they are speaking. See if your child can spot more subtle emotions, like anxiety, jealousy, surprise, fear or kindness.
• Sit together and write down some words with similar meanings to happy, sad and angry. How about 'cheerful' or 'joyous' for happy, 'glum' or 'gloomy' for sad, or 'furious' or 'annoyed' for angry? This activity will improve your child's emotional vocabulary.
• Using a mirror, have your child practice facial expressions that match these sentences: 'I don't understand', 'I'm really glad to see you', 'I didn't hear that', and 'I'm really mad you broke my toy'. Turn it into a game, and see if you can guess which sentence your child is showing you.

Making and keeping friends

Friendships are a vital part of your child's life, and provide more than just playmates. Friendships help children develop emotionally and morally. They enable children to practise controlling their emotions and responding to the emotions of others. Through friendships, children learn how to communicate, cooperat, and solve problems. Friendships even affect school performance; children tend to have better attitudes about learning at school when they have friends there.

23 Let's be friends...

Set aside some time to talk through the 'making friends' ideas with your child. Write 'good ideas' and 'not so good ideas' at the top of the paper, and place the ideas in the relevant column as your child decides. You should extend this activity by talking about his choices after the selection has been made. Ask your child why some ideas would work and some wouldn't, and why. Talk about any real-life examples of making friends.

Correct answers
✳ Stars – good ideas
▲ Triangles – not so good ideas
Score 1 point for each correct answer

How did it go?
Six or more correct answers show that your child understands the fundamental 'rules' about making friends and is well on the way to being people smart. These skills will be invaluable as he moves into adolescence and adulthood.

Five or less correct answers reveal that your child probably needs to reach out more to make friends. This takes courage because there is always the risk of rejection. Try to put a positive spin on any setbacks to boost your child's confidence, and talk about friendship on a regular basis.

Boosting activities
• Expand your child's circle of friends by inviting a child to play at your house. If your child is shy, arrange for a slightly younger child to visit so that your child gets a chance to lead. If your child is a bit bossy or has difficulty sharing, meet in a neutral place such as the park.
• Have your child make a 'social map'. Write his name in the middle of a page, and ask him to add the names of the people he is closest to (friends and family) near it. Then add the names of acquaintances he isn't as close to further away. Encourage your child to add as many friends as possible. Talk about the map together – are there people he would like to get to know better?

Relationship challenges

There are times when even strong relationships are strained, and an important people-smart skill is the ability to resolve any differences by finding satisfying solutions. Young children often react to relationship problems in ineffective ways, like crying, hitting another child or running to a parent. People-smart children approach problem-solving in a methodical way: they work out what the problem is, then come up with some ideas for solving it and finally, evaluate each idea to come up with the best plan.

24 What would you do if?

Set aside some time to talk through the scenarios on the card with your child. Make sure you are both relaxed and treat this activity more as a 'chat' than a test. Evaluate whether your child (a) understands the problem, (b) can come up with some plans to resolve it, and (c) thinks about the consequences of acting in a particular way, so that he arrives at the best plan of action. Talk about the pros and cons of each 'plan', and the consequences of putting it into action.

How did it go?
Did your child:
- Understand the activity?
- Enjoy discussing the various scenarios?
- Seem able to come up with ideas for problem-solving and conflict resolutions, and evaluate them thoughtfully?
- Really get into the spirit of the activity?
- Demonstrate an increased awareness of problem-solving or conflict resolution after the activity?

If the answer is 'Yes' to three or more of these questions, it reveals that your child is likely to be good at resolving conflicts, which is useful both in forming lasting friendships and in acting as a negotiator with peers.

If the answer is 'No' to three or more of these questions, then your child may be relying on immature methods of problem-solving, and he just needs to learn some alternatives that are more likely to bring a permanent peace.

Boosting activities
- Children learn the majority of their problem-solving skills from watching the adults in their lives interact. Include your child in any of the following family negotiations: which DVD to watch, where to go on Sunday, what to have for lunch, or who should have a friend to play.
- Problem-solving is helped by the ability to see the other person's perspective and anticipate his or her emotions – this is called empathy. You can promote empathy in your kids by encouraging them to volunteer their time to help others.

Social setbacks

We've all had times when we have felt rejected or tried to join a conversation and have been met with a frosty reception. Children experience this, too. Some children react angrily, and feel others are mean or 'out to get them', while other children withdraw and think they just aren't fun to be around. People-smart kids tend to view rejections as temporary or think they could have done something differently to improve the outcome. They recognise that the situation itself might have led to the rejection – if two children play with a truck each, they could find it difficult to include another in the game.

25 Why do things go wrong?

Set aside some time to talk through the scenarios on the card with your child. Make sure you are both relaxed and pick an informal location, so that your child feels you are having a conversation rather than being assessed. Look out for suggestions that are both external (to do with another child) and internal (to do with your child). You can extend the activity by talking about how your child might do things differently in each of the scenarios.

How did it go?
Did your child:
- Understand the activity?
- Seem able to relate to the various scenarios?
- Seem able to suggest both external and internal reasons for the other children's behaviour?
- Really get into the spirit of the activity?
- Demonstrate an increased ability to see social setbacks in a positive light?

If the answer is 'Yes' to three or more of these questions, your child is definitely people smart, and emotionally resilient and optimistic. She will find relationships easy and rewarding later on.

If the answer is 'No' to three or more of these questions, your child is probably too young at present to see the other person's side; this comes with maturity and age. Provide optimistic suggestions for social setbacks, to encourage your child to open up to new people.

Boosting activities
- To encourage your child to see the good in everyone, make a family 'praise box' from an old shoe box, decorating it together. Put it with pen and paper in a prominent place in your home. Encourage all family members to praise each other for something specific by writing a short note, and placing it in the box. Open the box once a week and take turns reading the notes.
- Read the children's story *Pollyanna*, by Eleanor H. Porter. Pollyanna plays the 'glad game', which is about finding a silver lining in every cloud, and she transforms the lives of those around her. See if you can play the 'glad game' in your family!

WHAT IS SELF SMART?

People who know themselves well and have a strong sense of who they are, their strengths and weaknesses, are self smart. These people think about, and learn from, past experiences. Developing this type of intelligence reinforces confidence, self-control and assertiveness, which lead to happy, stable relationships and success in life.

While it could be argued that it doesn't matter too much if someone doesn't exploit musical or artistic ability, understanding our emotional motivations is essential for every aspect of our lives. At the core of personal intelligence is the ability to think about and distinguish between feelings, to recognise them as discrete emotions and then use them to direct behaviour. This chapter includes tests on three aspects of self smart, each addressing a key area:

- **Who am I?** – an examination of temperament, the in-built aspect of character and personality.
- **Being myself** – recognising and taking ownership of feelings.
- **I can choose** – the difference between feelings and reactions, and choosing how and when to act on emotions.

ENCOURAGING PERSONAL INTELLIGENCE

Being self smart is your child's greatest key to success. When your child has completed the tests, you will both have a better idea of what she is good at and what she finds difficult. A great way of improving self smart is to help your child set goals. Goals can be big ('I want to be Prime Minister!') or small ('I want to finish reading my book'). They can be for things you want to do today ('I want to spend some time drawing') or in the future ('I want to learn to play the guitar'). The key

thing is that they are for specific things your child really cares about, and are realistic but challenging. Have your child set goals and review them regularly.

Emotional intelligence, which includes self smart, is learned from your child's home environment. Your child watches how you manage your own emotions and how you react to situations. You also may be inadvertently teaching your child how to deal with her feelings by how you coach her in expressing her emotions. Do you believe that girls shouldn't be 'pushy' or that boys shouldn't cry?

Whiz Kid

Harry Houdini

Born in Budapest, Hungary in 1874, Erik Weisz ran away from home when he was just 12 in order to earn money and seek adventure. He travelled around the country for about a year and then met his father in New York City. He was very athletic and won awards in swimming and track, building up the stamina and strength he needed to succeed as an escape artist. He was noted for his sensational performances – such as holding his breath inside a sealed milk can. Houdini's formal education was limited, but his self-education was immense. He was often quoted as saying 'My mind is the key that sets me free.'

HELPING YOUR CHILD WITH THE ACTIVITIES

The activities are best done in sequence, because each one builds on knowledge gained from the previous one. An understanding of temperament can be viewed as the foundation stone. This is followed by the recognition of feelings and learning to distinguish between them. Finally, once your child understands her feelings, she can begin to control them and think before acting on them.

The nature of the tests calls for your child to reveal personal information about herself. There are no right or wrong answers. You must respect your child's right to withhold things from you, or to discontinue the tests if she feels uncomfortable. Children need to feel that they are not being judged, or punished for giving a 'wrong' answer. It is possible that while doing a test your child may tell you something you weren't expecting or find upsetting. In this case, discontinue the test, and use the opportunity to gently question her about it. Don't panic; take time out to consider the best course of action.

WHAT TO LOOK FOR

Younger children may need some time to understand the tests, so make sure you talk through the ideas behind each one with your chilld before you start. Her responses may be a bit immature, because she is still learning about her feelings and how to deal with them. You could use the subject matter simply as a springboard for talking about feelings together as a family.

Talk about your own feelings openly to create a climate of trust.

Personality types

Everyone has natural inborn traits, which we call 'temperament'. Our temperament consists of attitudes, moods and inclinations, which affect how character and personality develop through childhood. Temperament depends on whether you use information from your five senses, listen to your inner voice, make decisions based on logic or make decisions based on emotions.

26 Who am I?

WANTED

Most children are a blend of the four personality types but will have one that is dominant. Helping your child discover her type enables her to learn about herself emotionally. Self-smart children and adults are aware of their temperament, and can play to its strengths and overcome its weaknesses.

Begin by introducing the idea of temperament and personality – that everyone has a natural inclination towards certain ways of thinking and behaving. You may need to talk about each statement so that you are sure your child understand what it means. You can extend the activity by choosing statements that apply to you, and discussing your temperament with your child.

How did it go?

Choosing the first and fifth statements indicates that your child depends on her senses, and is adaptable, practical and realistic. The weakness of a 'sensing' temperament is a tendency to live in the present, without learning from the past or anticipating the future.

Choosing the second and sixth statements indicates an that your child has a strong inner voice, and can detect patterns in information or behaviour. The weakness of an 'intuitive' temperament is to worry more about the future than the present, and a dislike of routine.

Choosing the third and seventh statements indicates your child has a strong sense of logic, and uses her intellect to evaluate things rationally. The weakness of a 'thinking' temperament is a tendency to seem cold and unemotional, and a difficulty in talking about feelings.

Choosing the fourth and eighth statements indicates your child is emotionally warm and has a strong sense of ethics, and of what is 'good' and 'bad'. The weakness of a 'feeling' temperament is a tendency to be emotionally manipulative and touchy or take things the wrong way.

If your child's three choices are from three different temperament types, your child has a blend of temperaments.

Boosting activities
• Talk about how someone from each temperament might feel or act differently. What sort of hobbies might they have? What sort of jobs might they do? An intuitive person might make a good counsellor; a sensing person might enjoy playing a musical instrument, for example.
• Have your child draw up a list of any decisions she has made today (like who she played with, and TV programmes he watched). What influenced those decisions, why did she act in the way she did? Think about the decisions in the light of your child's temperament type.

Understanding emotions

We all experience a wide range of emotions daily. Some are rare, some occur regularly. A key element of being self smart is the ability to recognise the feelings that can spring up inside us. Understanding emotions can help us express them, and once you know how you feel, you can start to understand why. Children often lack the emotional vocabulary to pinpoint uncomfortable feelings, which can lead to inappropriate reactions. But being able to name a feeling can help them handle it.

27 Being myself

Introduce the idea of emotions – that everyone has a range of feelings, which aren't right or wrong, or good or bad, and that they change. Talk about the meaning of each word and give examples, if necessary. You also could describe the physical sensations that go with some of these emotions – when you're angry you feel tense or hot, and when you're anxious you have butterflies in your tummy. You can extend the activity by taking part and discussing your feelings with your child.

How did it go?
Did your child:
• Understand the activity?
• Seem able to identify the emotions she experienced?
• Identify any other emotions not listed?
• Really get into the spirit of the activity?
• Demonstrate an increased awareness of her emotional range after the activity?
If the answer is 'Yes' to three or more of these question, it indicates that your child has good self-awareness, since identifying emotions is the first step in managing them. Self-smart people regularly think about how they are feeling, and use this insight to cope with difficult emotions.

If the answer is 'No' to three or more of these questions, then it may be because your child's emotional vocabulary is limited. Talk about what each of the words mean, and give examples that are relevant to her.

Boosting activities
• Help your child make a 'comfort box' for times when she feels sad and needs an emotional lift. Fill it with items that evoke good memories or are uplifting for your child – a holiday photo, a favourite music tape, an old cuddly toy, some of her favourite sweets, or a recipe for biscuits you can make together. Store the box until needed.
• Let your child choose one of the emotions (positive or negative) that she identified and linked with a particular incident. Talk about the actual events. Discuss what your child thought and felt. Ask questions like, 'What happened then?', 'What did you think?', 'How did that make you feel?' and 'How do you feel about it now?'.

Dealing with emotions

One of the skills self-smart people have is the ability to separate thoughts, feelings and reactions. This is hard to do, because in reality they often occur almost simultaneously – you are shouted at, you feel hurt, you shout back. It can be helpful to distinguish between these steps so you can stop yourself from acting before you have thought things through and examined your feelings and can plan the most effective response — which isn't usually isn't the first reaction that comes to mind.

28 I can choose

Read through each statement with your child and let her decide whether A and B are feelings or actions.

A great way of teaching your child about the difference is to use a traffic-light analogy. When something happens, she should see it as a red light, and stop and think about what the problem is. The 'light' will change to amber, so she can pause to put a name to herfeelings and plan the best course of action. When she is ready with her plan, then it's green for go. Emphasise the difference between a feeling (in your head) and an action (what you actually do). Score 1 point for each correct answer

Correct answers
1. (A) feeling; (B) action
2. (A) action; (B) feeling
3. (A) feeling; (B) action
4. (A) action; (B) feeling
5. (A) feeling; (B) action

How did it go?
If your child got five or more correct answers, she is able to make the distinction between feelings and actions, a key element of being self smart. Reinforce this ability by asking about actions and feelings in real life – it's much harder to stop and think in the heat of the moment.

Four or less correct answers show your child may need more coaching from you in the difference between feelings and actions. Talk over the statements on the card, and explain that what you think or feel about something is different from what you do about it.

Boosting activity
• Role play is a very successful technique for helping children deal with difficult situations, particularly those that crop up regularly. Discuss with your child what those situations are, and then re-enact them as you 'play' the other child. This will help your child prepare for difficult events and practice saying uncomfortable things.

WHAT IS NATURE SMART?

Naturalistic intelligence is the ability to nurture, identify and classify plants, animals, and natural phenomena. We all know people who are 'green fingered' and can grow and nurture plants, or those who have an incredible empathy with animals.

Children who are nature smart love being outdoors; they enjoy keeping pets, growing plants from seed, collecting fossils, reading nature books or watching TV shows on the natural world. They usually have an interest in 'exciting' species like dinosaurs or sharks.

There are two nature-smart tests in this book and they cover the two most important skills associated with naturalistic intelligence:

Observation – the ability to notice and interpret subtle changes in nature.

Classification – the ability to sort and classify natural objects by distinguishing between features.

ENCOURAGING NATURAL INTELLIGENCE AT HOME

Developing 'nature smartness' has a positive impact on other intelligences, too. Sorting a collection of feathers or rocks calls on thinking smart. Nurturing a pet or plant helps self smart. Working out the relationships between people, plants and animals in an ecosystem involves people smart. As many natural activities are done outdoors, there also are the physical and emotional health benefits of being out and at one with nature. So encouraging your child's nature smartness will help him grow as a person.

If you live near countryside, or in a rural area, you probably already take advantage of the great outdoors. It involves more planning and effort to get in touch with nature if you live in an urban environment. If you don't have a garden you can still keep a window box of flowers or herbs, or a few fish in a tank. Small mammals such as hamsters can live in a cage in a child's room. Try to visit parks or nature reserves in your free time, and take advantage of the knowledgeable guides who work there. Most cities have zoos, where you can see and learn about animals close up.

HELPING YOUR CHILD WITH THE ACTIVITIES

Keep in mind the purpose of the activity as you undertake it with your child: recognising powers of observation or the

Whiz Kid

Charles Darwin

Darwin was born in Shropshire, England in 1809. Even as a boy Darwin loved science and his enthusiasm for chemical studies earned him the name 'Gas' from his friends. He was also an avid collector of anything 'natural', which demonstrates his flair for nature smart.

In 1831, aged 22, he joined the survey ship, HMS Beagle as its naturalist. The round-the-world journey lasted almost five years, and throughout the journey, Darwin shipped back crate loads of tropical plants, insects, shells and fossil animals. On his return, Darwin studied his collections and notes from the voyage, and hit upon the idea of Natural Selection, the most widely accepted theory on evolution today.

ability to sort and classify. Overlook any other aspect, such as impatience, disorganisation, or messiness! You are looking for a real love of nature, and an enthusiasm for things in the natural world.

The nature-smart tests are quite time-intensive – we have to slow to nature's pace – so you won't get a quick answer about your child's abilities. It's best to plan these activities for a weekend, or in the school holidays, when you have plenty of time available. These are great projects for you to do together or even as a family; you may learn something yourself!

WHAT TO LOOK FOR

Young children may just not have the patience or concentration to stick with the tests; they tend to like quick results and to move swiftly onto the next thing that fires their enthusiasm. Do spend time doing the activities together with your child, because he is more likely to stick at something if he is receiving your full attention. Children are naturally curious, though, so keep things fresh and exciting by pointing out features he might miss.

Observing nature

Although nature smart can be difficult to tune into if you live in an urban environment, we all take notice of the weather, so it's a great way to encourage a key nature-smart skill – observation.

29 Weather watch

To assess your child's powers of observation in the natural world, help him write a weather diary. You will need a small notebook, a minimum/maximum temperature thermometer and a small measuring jug for catching rainfall. The diary can be as simple or as complicated as he wants – although it might be better to start with just a couple of measurements if you think your child might get bored with record-keeping. You could extend this activity by asking him to find out more about clouds – how they are formed and what the different formations mean.

How did it go?
Did your child:
• Understand the activities?
• Enjoy taking weather measurements?
• Seem able to take weather measurements and interpret findings with ease?
• Really get into the spirit of the activities?
• Demonstrate an increased interest in observing the weather?
If the answer is 'Yes' to three or more of these questions, then your child has excellent observation and classifying skills, which are fundamental to being nature smart. Build on these skills by observing nature and classifying other natural materials, like leaves or shells, together.
   If the answer is 'No' to three or more of these questions, then it could be because you need to build up your child's concentration by finding out what fires his enthusiasm.

Boosting activities
• Take up stargazing. Buy or borrow a book or star chart that shows the major constellations. Dress warmly, and lie on the ground together on a blanket. Using a flashlight to read the book or chart, see how many star groups you can find. Most children don't know that the signs of the zodiac can be found in the sky!
• Watch television nature programmes together and talk about what you see. Try National Geographic or the Discovery Channel.

Classifying nature

There is a lot going on in the natural world. If you look in just one corner of your garden, or a flower bed in the park, you'll see several plant species growing alongside one another, insects crawling or flying or spiders weaving their webs. These situations appear chaotic, but they are highly ordered, both in the natural way plants and animals live and grow, and in terms of the way scientists describe and classify living things. The ability to classify, to bring order and sense to an environmental situation, is another attribute of nature smart.

30 What's that tree?

Your child will create a collection of tree leaves and, with your help, identify and label each specimen. You will need a reference book on leaves (bought or borrowed from the library) or Internet access (there are tree-identification sites), a scrapbook for storing specimens, glue for fixing specimens, a pen and a camera (optional). You could extend this activity by making leaf rubbings (by placing the leaf under tracing paper and rubbing a crayon over the surface) or a leaf scrapbook (see page 20).

How did it go?
Did you child:
- Understand the activity?
- Enjoy collecting leaf samples?
- Seem able to notice slight differences in leaf formation?
- Really get into the spirit of the activity?
- Demonstrate an increased interest in collecting and classifying natural objects?

If the answer is 'Yes' to three or more of these questions, then your child has excellent observation and classifying skills, which are fundamental to being nature smart. Build on these skills by observing nature and classifying other natural materials, like leaves and shells, together.

If the answer is 'No' to three or more of these questions, then it could be because you may need to build up your child's concentration by finding out what fires his enthusiasm.

Boosting activities
- Plan a visit to a natural history museum, zoo or aquarium, and explore the different methods for classifying plants and animals that scientists use. Do you think they make sense? Can you think of other ways?
- Plant a tree in your garden or enrol your child in a tree-planting organisation such as Woodland Trust, who offer activities and information for children.

What's the pattern?

 Which of these belongs
with the others?

A mouse   B ball   C hat

 Which is the next picture in the sequence?

   ?

A   B   C

 If ...

what does ...   ?

A   B   C

 Which shape is the most
different from this one?

A   B   C

Brainstorming

Brainstorming means thinking up as many answers to a question as possible. Sometimes you may think of so many ideas it feels like there is a storm in your brain! Try these – you can be as crazy as you want!

1 What can you buy in a shop?

'We went to a shop and bought...'

2 What would you do if you were king or queen for a day?

'I would...'

3 Why didn't you do something you were supposed to?

'I didn't eat my lunch because...'

You can make your own secret messages by creating a code that only you and another person can understand. Write down all the letters of the alphabet, or just those letters in your name. Think of a different picture or symbol for all the letters.

Here's an example

I LOVE MOM

If your name was

MOLLIE

how would you write it in the code above?

Now try writing your own secret messages!

Changing shapes

Things aren't always what they appear to be!
Have a go at answering the following questions.

1 Which letter of the alphabet is this?

E? F? L?

2 Which one of these shapes (A, B or C) can you see in the picture?

A   B   C

3 Which of these designs is the 'odd one out'?

A   B   C

4 How many triangles are there in this picture?

1? 2? 3?

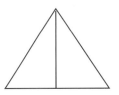

5 If you flattened out this cone, what shape would it be?

A   B   C

Smart art

Try doing one or all of these art projects:

 ## Patterns in nature

Collect examples of differently shaped and patterned items – shells, feathers, leaves, pinecones, flowers or tree barks. Present your collection on a tray, arranging your pieces carefully. Explain your collection to a grown-up.

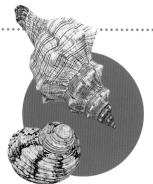

Face painting

First, plan what you will paint on scrap paper – for example, you could be a butterfly, a clown, a tiger or a super hero. Stand in front of a mirror and draw on your face using suitable paints, according to your plan. You could even paint your mum's face!

Seeing things differently

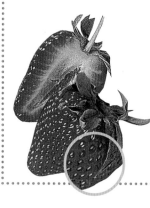

Pick a small object, like a strawberry, button or a bottle top. Draw it with a pencil. Look at the object again using a magnifying glass, and draw what you can see. Similarly, draw a distant object then look at it using binoculars or a telescope. How different do things look close up?

Do it in 3D!

Here are two ideas to transform your bedroom

 Mobile magic

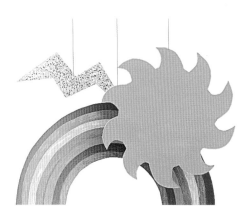

It's easy to use wire hangers and decorated paper cutouts or your own special objects to make a mobile. Think about how the mobile will look from every angle, including from below. Imagine it finished in your head, and draw a plan to remind yourself of how you want it to look. Will it have a theme, like the weather, sport or the planets, or will you choose objects that match your room's colour scheme? Use thread to fix each object to the hangers.

 Bedroom remix

To give your bedroom a new look, rearrange the furniture. Imagine where you could move the items, thinking about the space you need to work or play, and the location of the door and windows. Draw a plan of your room, and cut out shapes to scale to represent your bed, storage, desk, chairs and so on. When you decide on your final plan, check it with a parent, and get his/her help to move things around the way you want them.

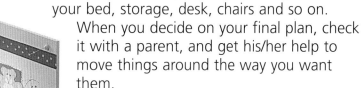

Amazing mazes

You are going to try and find your way out of two mazes.

'Enter' this maze at the arrow. See if you can 'get out' without making any wrong turns!

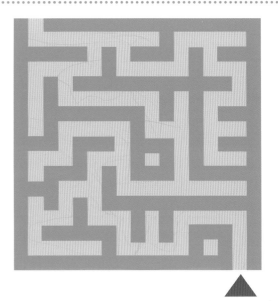

With this maze, you also 'enter' at the arrow but you want to end up in the centre.

Letters and sounds

1 Write these sentences correctly
A is My green. coat

B dog run. A can

2 Fill in the missing letters:
A d_ck

B sh_e

3 Choose the rhyming words
A red

B look

C took

D bed

4 Which of these words are clothes you can wear?
A hat B nap

C sock D bowl

E tick

5 Try these word sums
A d + ow + n = ?

B f + a + ll = ?

All about me!

You are going to put together a scrapbook all about yourself, using writing to explain the pictures and other items you might use.

1. Think about how you would describe yourself and the things that are important to you. You might want to include your family, pets, school, holidays, likes and dislikes, hobbies, favourite things and friends.

2. Collect pictures, photos and anything you can stick in a scrapbook that describes you in some way.

3. Decide on the words that go with every picture, like 'My brother loves cooking!' with a photo of him in the kitchen, or "'My favourite football team is Liverpool' with an old ticket.

4. Ask a parent for help with writing if you need to, but remember – YOU get to decide on what to say!

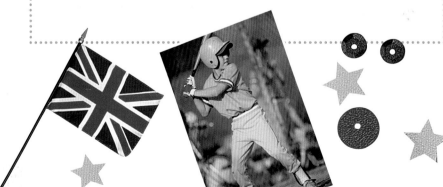

Try a talking game

1 Under my bed

The first player starts by saying, 'I looked under my bed and found a...' and then makes up something he found, like 'a puppy'. The next player says, 'I looked under my bed and found a puppy and ..." and then adds a second item, like 'a tennis racket'. Now take turns to add to the list. Start again when the list becomes too long!

2 Cooperation story

This game involves making up a story together. Start by saying 'One day I was playing in the garden when ...'. The next player adds to the story, ending with something exciting or unusual, like 'an enormous flying saucer came out of the sky and ...'. See how crazy and funny you can make the story!

3 Watch your back!

Cut out lots of pictures of items or animals from magazines or catalogues. Get another player to choose a picture, and stick it to your back with tape. You have to try to guess what it is. Ask for clues if you get stuck. Take turns to be the 'guesser'.

Party animals

1 Who has the most balloons, the rabbit or the monkey?

2 How many pieces of fruit are in the bowls?

3 How many presents were there to start with if four have already been opened?

4 How many straws are in the cups?

5 How many sandwiches have been eaten if there were twelve to start with?

Candy and counting

1 How much money do you have to spend?

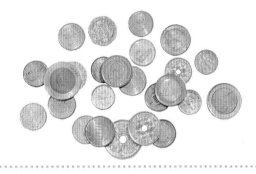

2 What have you decided to buy?

3 How much will you have to pay?

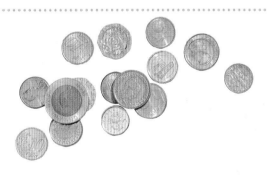

4 How much money will you have left?

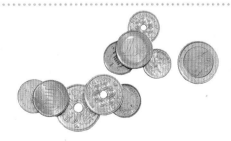

You are going to search for numbers. See how many you can find either inside your home or outdoors.

Write down all the different places you found numbers.

To get you started, look at the numbers on this card. Can you work out where they came from and what they mean?

Cut, stick and construct

1 Make a model

Build a robot, dinosaur, or fairy-tale castle.

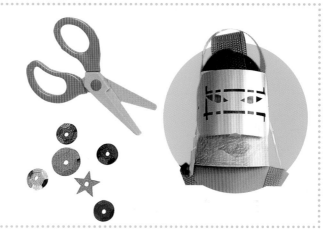

2 Paint a picture

Create a portrait of your mum or dad or of yourself.

3 Construct a collage

Paste pasta and dried peas and beans on paper to make a pattern.

Move your body

Actors use their entire bodies to communicate feelings to their audiences. You are going to mime (that means acting without speaking or making any sounds) some animals and people. See if your audience can guess what or who you are pretending to be … but remember, no talking!

A dog

Get down on all fours, sniff around, wag your tail, and dig up a bone!

A musician playing the drums

Sit on a chair, and use your hands and feet to pretend you are playing a drum kit.

A kangaroo

Pretend you are jumping along in the bush, eating some leaves, and looking after the joey (baby kangaroo) in your pouch.

A fisherman

Cast your line then act as if you are reeling in a huge fish. Then show your audience how big it is!

Yoga zoo

Yoga is an exercise that improves your flexibility, and gets your brain and body working together. It's also fun to do. Yoga postures often are named after animals, reflecting the different shapes your body can make. You are going to do two, the cat and the cobra (a snake).

The Cat

Begin on your hands and knees. Keep your hands just in front of your shoulders, your legs about hip-width apart. Breathe in and let your spine dip down and your bottom tilt up. Gently lift your head and look straight ahead. Then, breathe out and round your back, pushing your bottom down, and curling your chin in towards your chest. Repeat as often as you like.

The Cobra

Lay on your stomach with your legs together and place your hands flat slightly in front of you. Breathe in, straighten your arms, and slowly raise your head and chest as high you can, making sure you look straight ahead. Breathe in and out several times and then lower yourself down. Repeat as often as you like.

Balancing act

Here are some fun activities that will test your balance. Get your parent to help you set them up. You could do them on your own or with friends.

 Circus tightrope

How far can you walk without 'falling off'?

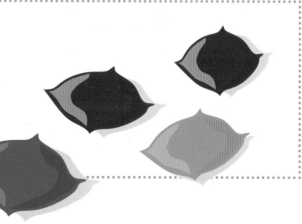

2 **Sack race**

How far can you jump without falling over?

3 **Pirate treasure**

Escape back to your 'pirate ship' without dropping the treasure!

4 **Crossing the river**

Jump on the 'rocks' so you don't fall in the water!

Musical pitch is about what note a sound is – high or low. You are going to play a game where you have to guess whether two notes are the same or different.

1 Fill three glasses with different amounts of water.

2 Turn your back so you can't see the glasses and ask an adult to play one 'note' followed by another.

3 Say whether you think the note is the same or different.

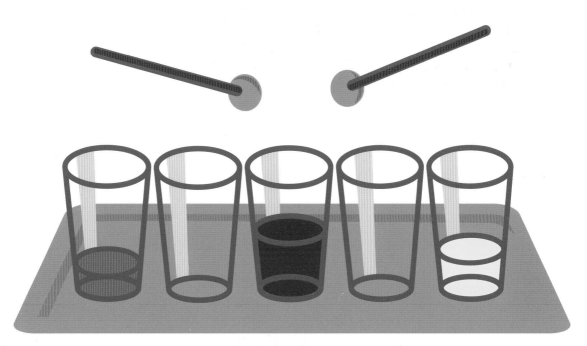

It can be fun making up new words, or lyrics, to well-known tunes. Try writing a new song to the tune of 'Frère Jacques' (also known as 'Are you sleeping, Brother John?'). Think about the number of beats in the rhythm, and remember that the words at the end of the lines should rhyme.

You can write about anything – your favourite sports star 'John plays football ...' or something you like eating, 'I love ice-cream ...' – whatever you like!

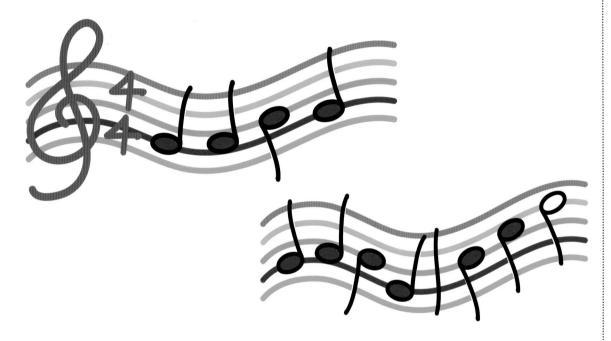

Here's an example:

'I hear thunder, I hear thunder,

Can you too? Can you too?

Pitter patter rain drops, Pitter patter rain drops,

I'm wet through, So are you!'

Feel the music

Music can make us experience many different emotions. You are going to listen to two pieces of music. Think about how each one makes you feel. Then listen to them again, and talk about your feelings with an adult.

1 Do you think the music is trying to make you feel a certain way?

2 How do you feel when you listen to it?

3 How do the words (if there are any) work with the music?

4 Is the music telling a story?

5 Does the music remind you of anything – other songs or things that happened to you? Why?

Rubber-band violin

21

You are going to make a simple 'violin' and 'bow'.

1 Take an empty tissue box and place five rubber bands on the box so that they cross the opening.

2 Make your bow by stretching a rubber band over a pencil, from the eraser end to the tip, which should not be sharpened.

3 Now play your violin

- **Play each band with your bow.**
  Do they all sound the same or are there differences?

- **Pluck each band with your fingers.**
  Does it sound different to using your bow?

- **Experiment using rubber bands of different lengths and thicknesses on your violin.**
  What are the differences in sound?

- **Press your finger down on one band on top of the tissue box.**
  What happens to the note the band produces?

- Play a tune!

We all use our voices to speak, to say words to communicate with other people.

But did you know that we use our voices in different ways depending on how we feel?

For this game, you are going to guess whether an adult is

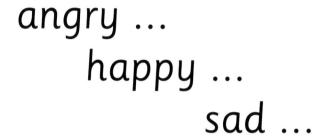

just by his or her voice!

Angry?

Happy?

What made you choose your answer?

How could you tell?

Sad?

Let's be friends ...

Everyone needs friends but making new friends can be hard, especially if you are shy or have just moved to a new neighbourhood. Below are some ideas that can help you make friends and some that won't. You decide which are the good ideas and which are not so good.

* Smile at someone.

▲ Pretend you are rich so people will like you.

* Suggest a game that another person can play.

* Find something to talk about that might interest somebody else.

▲ Walk away while someone is talking to you.

* Think of a way someone can play with you if he or she is on their own.

▲ Talk about yourself without asking the other person anything.

* Join a club for people with the same interests as you.

▲ Stand on your own and don't talk to anyone.

What would you do if?

24

Do you ever argue with kids at school, or members of your family? Having disagreements isn't a bad thing in itself, but if you can't solve the issue it can really get you down.

Here are some difficult situations you might find yourself in. Think about all the different ways you might react. What's the best thing to do – and why?

- You and your brother or sister both want the last piece of pizza.

- You are playing with a toy and another child tries to take it from you.

- Your mother lets you wear her watch and you break it.

- You share something with a friend, but he or she refuses to give it back.

- Your teacher tells you off for something you didn't do.

Making friends isn't always easy. You may have asked a friend to come over and play and he or she said 'Sorry, I can't.' You probably felt hurt, but there might have been a good reason why he or she couldn't come. For example, your classmate might have been busy on that day, or might have felt sad because he or she had a bad day at school, or you might not have smiled or seemed very friendly. What do you think may be behind the following situations:

- You ask if you can eat lunch with a group of children at school, and they say 'No.'

- You see two friends talking together, but when you join them the conversation stops.

- You normally sit next to your next-door neighbour on the school bus, but this morning he or she was sitting with someone else.

Who Am I?

Would you like to find out about what sort of person you are? For example, are you someone who enjoys making things, or are you more interested in being with people? The statements below can help you learn more about yourself – the things you like, and the things you don't. Choose the three you think most apply to you. You can talk about them with a grown-up, if you like.

I enjoy activities that use one of my senses like bird-watching, listening to music, cooking or making craft objects.

I get 'hunches' about things, and trust my instincts.

I love discovering new facts about things.

I am interested in people and their feelings.

I like to think about what's going on right now, not what has already happened or might happen in the future.

I'm happy doing new and unusual things.

I think there should be a good reason behind everything.

I'm able to affect how other people feel – when I'm in a good mood, other people start to feel happy, too.

WANTED

Being myself

How are you feeling right now? Worried? Excited? If you can recognise and understand your feelings, it can help you feel better and understand more about yourself. You can make the most of good feelings, and make bad feelings a little easier to get over.

Here are some words that describe feelings. Which have you felt in the last day? Did something happen to make you feel that way? Can you think of any other feelings you have had?

Angry	Nervous
Loving	Thrilled
Sad	Lonely
Ashamed	Proud
Annoyed	Worried
Embarrassed	Jealous
Happy	Frightened
Amazed	Caring

I can choose

In order to 'do the right thing', it is important to separate feelings from actions. When something occurs that hurts your feelings or makes you angry, you probably find it difficult to think straight. Here are five common situations along with a 'feeling' and an 'action' — which is which?

 Your friend moves away to a different county.

A You *feel sad.*

B You ask for the new address so you can stay in touch.

 You break your sister's or brother's favourite toy.

A You offer to fix it.

B You *feel guilty.*

 You wake in the night and hear a strange noise.

A You *feel scared.*

B You go into your mum's room to tell her.

 Your team wins a sports tournament.

A You phone your grandparents to share the good news.

B You *feel happy.*

 Your friend doesn't want to play with you anymore.

A You *feel sad.*

B You ask him or her why.

Weather watch

You can learn a great deal about nature by keeping track of the weather. If you note down your daily weather, you'll start to see patterns, and you might be able to make predictions, like a real weather forecaster!

Every day for at least two weeks, write an entry in your 'weather diary', a small notebook used for the purpose. Use a thermometer to measure temperature and a measuring jug to capture rainfall. You could include all or any of these ideas in your diary:

• The maximum temperature during the day.

• The minimum temperature at night.

• The daily rainfall amount.

• Is it sunny or cloudy? What do the clouds look like?

• Is it windy? What direction is the wind coming from?

Can you see any relationships between different aspects of weather or unusual changes in the weather? You could compare your actual weather with a real weather forecast on the TV, Internet or in the newspaper.

What's that tree?

Outside, all around you, are lots of different types, or species, of trees. You probably know the names of some trees, but did you know you can find out the name of any tree by studying a leaf and looking at how it grows?

1. Collect a number of different tree leaves. Notice the way the leaves grow on the tree – are they exactly opposite one another, or are they staggered, alternating on each side of the twig? Make a drawing to show the way the leaves are growing and the pattern of the veins in the leaf. You could even take a photo of the tree.

2. Using your samples and notes, look up your leaf in a reference book or on the Internet (ask a grown-up to help you with this).

3. Fix your leaf, photograph (if you have one) and your drawing to a scrapbook, and label your samples.

4. Keep adding to your collection until you have classified ten or more trees.

The Activities

These cover subjects that children find exciting and motivating and feed into areas of learning your child will discover at school, but more importantly, are those he needs for a fulfilled and well-rounded life. They also relate to the subjects 'tested for' in the book.

What areas are explored?
Although the activities deal with the natural world; history, science, legends and myths; they also help your child explore and encourage following general areas of learning such as language and literacy, maths, technological knowledge and exploration, creativity and personal, social and emotional intelligence.

Performing the activities
Again, as with the tests, you can choose to let your child pick an activity (from a pre-selected handful) and either work from the book, photocopy it to hand to your child or even cut it out.

The activities all have three steps.

Step 1 is to introduce the subject. This is your 'way into the activity', and it helps you to find out what your child already knows, so you can start an appropriate level. If your child finds the activity is too hard, he will become discouraged and switch off. If he thinks it is too easy, he will find the experience patronising and also will lose interest in the activity.

Step 2 is the making, investigating or experimenting part of the activity and is the most active part of the learning experience.

Step 3 encourages you to review with your child what he has done. Without evaluation, it is hard to improve upon and adapt the things we learn.

Each part of each activity has been given a suggested time-scale while the resources you need for each one are set out at the top of each card.

ABOUT THE ACTIVITIES

31 Learn the parts of a plant

This activity introduces your child to the biology of green plants in simple terms that he can understand. Your child can learn about the external parts of a plant in a practical way, by looking at a living plant. Encourage your child to look at the plant parts with a magnifier if you have one, looking closely at leaves to see the veins. Tell your child that the veins are like tubes that carry water and goodness to the leaves.

Cutting out the parts of the plant from felt will help your child to become more skilled with scissors, although he may need help as cutting felt is more challenging than cutting paper.

Boosting activity

Compare other types of flower, such as dandelions, with the daisy. How is the flower different? Look at the centre of different flowers, including composite flowers such as cow parsley or elderflowers, looking closely at the tiny flowers that make up the large flower we see.

32 Discover where bugs live

Bug hunting is a great adventure for children, who often feel none of the 'yuck factor' felt by adults! This activity should be treated like a safari – it may be on a small scale, but who knows what you will find? It is worth scouting around the park or garden yourself, looking for bugs to identify and their likely hiding places such as crevices in walls, under stones, etc.

The activity introduces your child to nature study and biological science in simple terms that he or she can understand.

Making a 'lift-the-flap book' (*see also page 20*) will encourage your child's creativity and gives her the opportunity to develop fine motor skills needed for drawing the creatures and cutting out the flaps to make the book.

Boosting activity

Make a pitfall trap together to see what lives in your garden or windowbox. Dig a small hole and sink a yogurt pot in the ground or soil. Cover the top to keep the creatures that fall in safe from the sun and predators such as birds. Place two small rocks on either side of the pot and rest a piece of board on top. This leaves a gap for creatures to wander in. Bait the trap with a piece of apple and a chunk of cheese, and leave it for a few hours. Come back and look at what you have caught. Use a field guide to identify the bugs.

33 Fashion an aquarium

Talking about what aquaria are made from, and looking at real aquaria will make your child consider why certain materials are used to create particular things – they have properties that are essential such as glass being used for the sides for an aquarium, because it is see through (transparent) so you can observe the sealife inside. This consideration of materials and their properties is something that will be taught in school science, where 'materials' is a topic, as well as design technology.

Finding out about sea creatures to make as occupants of the aquarium involves research on the Internet and in books – a valuable skill at any age.

Actually making the aquarium and its occupants will require your child to draw, cut and stick, and this will help to develop his artistic abilities. Talking about what he did in a review session will develop your child's skills in public speaking.

Boosting activity

Allow your child to keep some 'sea monkeys' – available very cheaply from pet shops – to study small marine creatures. He could keep a diary of their habits.

34 Go pond dipping

Pond dipping is an activity that fascinates children of all ages. Obviously, you need to emphasise that your child should not go near water without an adult, but supervised it is a safe and interesting activity.

Consulting a field guide is a useful scientific skill for nature study. Discussing the plants and creatures found in and around the pond will make your child familiar with the idea that different creatures and plants live in different habitats; this is an important concept. Finding out about the lifecycles of the creatures will further engage your child.

Making a memories book or display will help to embed in your child's memory the knowledge gained.

Boosting activity

Create a 3D pond model, using a strip of blue or green card rolled into a cylinder as the 'pond'. Add creatures – seen when pond dipping – made from modelling clay.

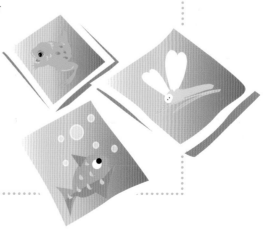

35 Sensory woodland walk

Looking at field guides together – even if your child is really young and cannot read the text – gets him into the habit of using the system, which will help him to use field guides independently later on.

Walking in the woods and taking time to look through binoculars and magnifiers will help your child to develop an appreciation of the natural world. Peering closely at plants and bugs prepares your child for biology lessons – and of course, it's fun!

Making a bed for the toy chosen will give you the opportunity to talk about animal life and what animals need to survive (food, water, shelter) – once again, feeding into the science learning your child will experience at school.

Boosting activity
Make a record of the walk with photos and found objects, such as leaves, seeds, etc., taped to a piece of card and displayed on the wall.

36 Compile a leaf diary

This science activity promotes an interest in the natural world and the way it works. It gives your child an insight into why leaves change colour in the autumn, as the tree absorbs chlorophyll from its leaves before they are shed.

Taking photos of the tree will encourage your child to develop skills in art, as will the replication of leaf colours by colour mixing. Creating a leaf diary is a great keepsake, as well as giving your child a chance to develop skills in recording the results and findings of investigations – a crucial scientific skill.

Boosting activity
Collect a variety of leaves as they fall and make them into bookmarks by drying them and capturing them between a piece of coloured card and sticky contact paper.

37 Create a window box farm

This activity will give your child a simple idea about how food is produced and where it comes from – geographical skills. Thinking about where in the world food comes from before it gets to our tables, also gives your child an early introduction to the ideas that are built upon in global studies.

The activity will also help your child learn about how things grow, introducing him to science concepts such as how seeds germinate and what plants need to stay healthy. With discussion, it will give him an appreciation of how we rely on the natural world for our food.

'Harvesting' the food will give your child a real sense of achievement, and he may like to have a patch in the garden if it is possible to grow longer term, 'child-friendly' high-interest plants such as tomatoes, pumpkins and sunflowers.

Boosting activity

Encourage your child to prepare a snack using the food he has grown, taking the chance to talk about healthy eating and the importance of eating five fruits and vegetables a day.

38 Construct a seasons mobile

This activity will encourage your child to consider the seasonal changes that take place in the natural world. It also will help to reinforce the order of the seasons, which young children sometimes find hard. Making the mobile gives your child the opportunity to draw detailed pictures and practise pencil control.

Organising the seasons into the correct order will help your child to learn about sequencing. Children of this age need a great deal of reinforcement and practise to learn this early mathematical skill, which is the basis of learning to count.

Helping to construct the mobile itself is a good design technology experience for this age group, including simple joining techniques such as using tape to make the cylinder.

Boosting activity

Your child could make a concertina book (made by folding paper in half and then folding each half backwards then forwards and securing with a ribbon tied round the book) of the seasons to help to reinforce the sequencing aspect of the activity.

39 Make a starfish badge

When you visit the aquarium, be sure to mention the way the creatures look, talking about legs, antennae, colour and skin texture. Models of creatures can also be used to explore the characteristics of the creatures, giving your child the opportunity to handle them. Many aquariums also run sessions at the 'touch pool', where children can stroke and gently handle live creatures such as crabs and anemones.

Making the badge will give your child the chance to explore different artistic methods such as painting and collage. Cutting out the shape of the badge will help your child to develop fine motor skills. Using both glue and tape as the badge is made gives you the opportunity to talk about the way things are joined together – a crucial skill for design technology.

Explaining the steps needed to make the badge will help to develop your child's ability to recall events and will help him learn to sequence things skills, which assists in the development of mathematical skills.

Boosting activity

Make a sealife bracelet by cutting out shapes in the same way as for the badge, perhaps alternating a pattern of shiny sweet-wrapper fish and starfish. Make a strip of card big enough to slip over your child's hand, and glue the sealife into place.

40 Create a dinosaur puppet

All children like dinosaurs. This natural enthusiasm is harnessed in this fun activity, designing and making a dinosaur finger puppet.

Find out what your child knows already by talking in general terms about dinosaurs. Use the books to find out more, and encourage your child to make sketches. This will help to develop your child's research skills. Comparing sizes of dinosaurs will help your child to develop the ability to estimate – an important mathematical skill. The thinking involved in designing and sketching the puppet will develop your child's design technology capability. Talking about the properties of the materials used will give your child vocabulary for art, science and technology. Practise in cutting out the dinosaur shape will help to develop your child's fine motor skills.

Boosting activity

Suggest your child makes other puppets and a backdrop for the puppets to 'act' in front of. She could also make a papier mâché landscape for his dinosaur puppets to roam across, complete with egg carton volcanoes and tin foil lakes.

41 Make a dinosaur mobile

The research involved in this activity, on the Internet and in books, will give your child practice at finding out information – a skill needed for all areas of learning. Talking about the dinosaurs, and what they may have been like, will develop your child's capacity for speaking and listening, and will help to build his concentration span as well as his scientific knowledge.

Drawing, painting and cutting out the dinosaurs will develop your child's artistic skills and will give him practice in working with a range of tools such as scissors and brushes.

Boosting activity

Make a dinosaur-shaped fact-file book about your child's favourite dinosaur. The cover could be made 3D by padding it out with layers of card cut to the same shape as the favoured dinosaur, the shapes becoming smaller and smaller with each layer (*see also* *page 21*).

42 Hatch some dinosaur eggs

This activity will help your child to think about how ideas are formulated, tested and proven. Talk to him about how scientists and palaeontologists formulated the idea that dinosaurs laid eggs: they looked at reptiles and lizards, the living relatives of the dinosaurs, and even birds, also related, and they all lay eggs. Fossils found looked like eggs; they even found fossils of hatching eggs. The fossils are the evidence that helped to prove the ideas.

Making the eggs is a fun art-and-craft activity. It will help your child to follow instructions, including the 'recipe' for the egg cases.

Boosting activity

Make a model of a baby dinosaur from modelling clay before putting it inside a home-made egg case.

43 Stock a story chest

This activity encourages storytelling, which will help your child to develop literacy skills. Make sure your child has plenty of experience of fairytales, looking at books with you and visiting the movies or theatre to see productions on a fairytale theme. This experience will be invaluable in developing her understanding of how stories 'work' – how there is a beginning, middle and end, and usually a conflict to be resolved.

Making the story chest will fire your child's imagination and develop her creativity and artistic abilities. Painting and decorating the chest will help her to develop fine motor skills. Talking about the items to go inside the chest will help your child to become knowledgeable about the items and characters found in fairytales, and will even help her to develop a sense of history as you talk about life in the past.

Building up your child's vocabulary to include a variety of adjectives as she describes the characters in the story will help your child's language development.

Boosting activity
You could have a family storytelling session where your child becomes involved in a communal story. Each family member takes a turn to build parts of the story, each following on from the one before. Grandparents can be especially skilled at this!

44 Make a mermaid/merman

Mermaids appear in myths from many cultures. Try to read your child a variety of mermaid stories and show him lots of pictures. This cultural activity will help your child to develop the beginning of a sense of common stories shared around the world; this type of idea needs to be added to and reinforced many times as children grow older.

The art activity – collaging, painting and drawing – will give your child the opportunity to explore a variety of artistic techniques and experiences. Provide a variety of materials for the activity, and encourage your child to choose the materials she uses according to their properties i.e. popping plastic, painted with a paint and PVA mix would make good seaweed as it has the right texture.

Boosting activity
Make a mermaid family to continue the theme, or even underwater 'pets' such as crabs and fish. Once again, encourage your child to think about the texture of the creature he is creating and how it matches with the materials available.

45 Construct pirate people

This art-and-craft activity will develop your child's skills in cutting, sticking and drawing. It will also encourage the development of her creativity as new characters are thought up, such as a parrot or a pirate ship's cat!

The characters can be used to act out plays, which will stimulate your child's imagination and encourage language development as your child creates dialogue for her 'actors'. This also can encourage storytelling, as your child makes up adventures for the pirate people.

Talk to your child about real pirates – look for pictures of characters such as Blackbeard and Anne Bonney in books and websites. Help your child to understand that pirates were a real danger for travellers on ships in the past.

Boosting activity
Your child could record the adventures of the pirate people as a comic strip. Draw a grid of six squares on a piece of A4 paper, fill in the squares with a simple 'cartoon' storyline and help your child to number the boxes 1–6 in sequence (which will help with her maths skills).

46 Fly a Jolly Roger

Looking for images of the Jolly Roger and finding out about how and when the flag was used will introduce your child to historical research. His design skills will be developed as your child sketches out and chooses materials for the flag. Cutting and sticking will help him to develop artistic and technological skills.

Acting as pirates will engage your child's imagination and he can even re-enact tales read as part of her research.

Boosting activity
Have your child write a pirate poem about the flag and the adventures it has on the high seas!

47 Create a captain's cutlass

This art-and-craft activity will help your child to develop skills such as using scissors for accurate cutting, and employing a template.

Looking at books and websites to find out about pirates will help your child to become used to carrying out research generally; in this instance with a historical flavour. Talking about how the cutlass was held and used will bring history to life, and making a facsimile artefact will help your child to imagine what real life as a pirate was like.

Writing instructions is an important skill in developing literacy; it is writing for a purpose, to explain how something is done. Non-fiction writing is an important part of your child's development as a writer.

Boosting activity

Encourage your child to use the information found out about pirates to write a play about a pirate adventure – which can then be acted out, using her cutlass as a prop!

48 Make a pirate boot clip

This activity encourages your child to develop designing and making skills, such as drawing, cutting and joining.

Finding out about pirates will develop her research skills, and will promote an interest in historical research in particular as he finds out about the wild seafaring life of the pirates!

Writing out instructions – writing for a purpose – will help your child to develop the ability to put things down clearly and concisely, which will be useful throughout his school years.

Boosting activity

Your child could make a matching coat hanger for his raincoat by adding a similar laminated 'head' – perhaps of the pirate cat this time – to a standard coat hanger. The picture can be taped or glued to the coat hanger, just beneath the hook.

49 Capture a fairy!

This activity will give your child the chance to imagine what it would be like to find real fairies. Talk to your child about the Cottingley Fairies case – does she believe that the fairies found there were real? (Do you?)

Modelling the fairy from clay will give your child the chance to experience fine, small-scale artwork. Finding out about fairies will increase her ability to carry out research and increase her knowledge of mythology. Explaining the habits and power of fairies gives your child the opportunity to speak to an audience – valuable for all areas of learning. Writing instructions gives your child practice in chronological, non-fiction writing, which is useful for future school subjects such as design technology and science.

Boosting activity
Your child could adapt the idea to make another 'captured' creature – what about a captured alien, hobgoblin or sprite?

50 'Dig up' the past

This activity is a great introduction for little ones to the fascinating world of the ancient Egyptians – a period your child will learn about in history classes at school. Apart from the historical aspects of the activity, your child will be using his artistic skills, in creating an interesting desert scene. Encourage your child to think about the way sand dunes look in a desert, and the vegetation that might be seen. Look for pictures on the Internet and in photographic books about Egypt at the library. Show your child on a globe or in an atlas where Egypt is found, to encourage the development of geographical skills.

Boosting activity
If you have a sandbox in the garden, hide toys in it for your child to find – let him pretend to be an archaeologist. You could extend this by buying cheap trinkets associated with ancient Egypt that your child has seen during a visit to a museum. Scarabs, pieces of papyrus and model mummies usually can be bought in 'pocket money' sections of the shop. Bury these, together with a few modern items, in the sand and ask your child to tell you which items could be from ancient Egypt.

51 Make a mummy book

This activity will develop the ability to carry out organised historical research via books and websites. It also will allow your child to see that belief systems (such as what happens after death) change over time and in different places.

Making the book will involve your child's creative skills as she designs and decorates the pages and the cover. Talking about the way in which mummies were made will develop your child's ability to organise presentations and 'show and tell', and this will help to develop your child's confidence.

Boosting activity

Make a cat-shaped mummy book. Cats were sacred animals in ancient Egypt and were often mummified along with pharaohs. Your child may like to write a story from the cat's point of view for the inside of the book.

52 Model an Egyptian mask

Making this mask is quite complex, but it will give your child the opportunity to develop a variety of skills. First of all, your child will carry out research. This ability is needed for learning in all areas of a school's curriculum, and indeed for life in general.

Moulding the shape of the face for the mask, by observing her own face, will increase your child's observational skills. Then your child covers the mask in papier mâché, another art and craft technique. Decorating the mask introduces another medium – either collage or painting, so your child will encounter a variety of artistic experiences by making this mask.

Giving a presentation will build your child's confidence and help him to speak confidently in public.

Boosting activity

Your child could make a collection of 'artefacts', such as clay canopic jars, facsimile papyrus pictures (from paper maché) and card and collage jewellery to display with the mask in her own 'ancient Egyptian museum'.

53 Let's go exploring

This activity is all about firing up your child's imagination! When you are building the den, you can make it as simple or as complicated as you like. At this age, a blanket over a table is as good as an elaborate den made from packing cases. This activity will develop your child's creative thinking and verbal skills, as he 'sees' the place in his mind's eye and describes it.

Give your child space to come up with ideas, but don't be afraid to make gentle suggestions and prompts. Join in wholeheartedly – clamber through the 'swamp' and hack your way through the 'jungle' together. When you are looking at pictures together, discuss the things you might 'see'; this will help develop your child's sense of place, and give her information about different habitats, which will be useful when studying science and geography.

Boosting activity

Can your child think of a different scenario to explore – perhaps the poles? With a few cuddly penguins and white bears and an anorak, your child could be an arctic explorer!

54 Map a 'lost' city

Your child's imagination will be fired by this activity! Describing the features of a fantastic 'lost city' will help your child to develop storytelling skills, while making the map will encourage your child's artistic abilities as she makes use of paint, pens and collage materials. Thinking about making an ancient document – the map – will make your child think about what historical artefacts look like, and may awaken her interest in history and archaeology.

Boosting activity

Make some artefacts for the 'lost city' treasure, such as plastic bottles covered with sweet wrappers or wrapping paper to look like precious containers, coins from metallic paper and necklaces with large 'jewels' from card and glitter, etc. You also can add junk jewellery items and old books to the hoard.

55 Learn about wind power

Try to do this activity on a windy day – it's so much easier if the effects of the wind are immediately obvious! Encourage your child to observe the wind's effects; he may even like to take photographs. Be ready to point out anything your child does not notice.

When you come back inside, use the toy windmill and bubbles. Emphasise that wind has the power to make things move – an important concept for science and geography. Playing the cloud game helps to reinforce the point – and makes science learning fun.

Discussing the way that the variation of conditions (i.e. flapping the paper faster) can affect the outcome is a great way to introduce your child to scientific testing and predictive thinking: 'What if...?'

If at all possible, take your child to see wind turbines, and talk about the way that the blades turn and produce electricity. Keep it simple; your child does not need to know how it happens at this stage – he just needs to be introduced to the idea.

Boosting activity

Make a collection of toys that use moving air to work, such as plastic hopping toys with a compressible bulb or 'stamp on' foam rockets.

56 Does it float or sink?

This activity is great fun – and it also introduces your child to the science topic 'floating and sinking', which he will revisit at various times during his school life. Children often have the simplistic idea that anything heavy will sink and everything light will float. This is not true (think of large metal ships) and avoid reinforcing this idea; when children learn science misconceptions they will have to unlearn them later – and that can be hard work!

Things float due to upthrust – the water pushing back up on items placed in water. A flat-bottomed plasticine boat with high sides will float (due to the large surface area pressing down on the water and the upthrust of the water on the 'boat') but a ball of plasticine weighing the same amount will sink as the upthrust against the smaller surface area is not great enough. Try out this experiment with a ball of plasticine and then demonstrate it to your child.

This activity can also serve as an introduction to the maths topic of capacity if you experiment with filling the bowl with jugs of water – how many jugs of water does your child estimate it will take to fill the bowl?

Boosting activity

Make a model boat that floats from a margarine tub and investigate how many marbles can be added to the tub before it sinks. Can your child make predictions about the number it will take?

57 Turn a liquid to a solid

This activity is about the science topic of changes. Although making lollies is simple, it gives you the opportunity to talk about states of matter (but obviously not using the term) – in other words, whether a material is a solid, a liquid or a gas. Your child will need lots of practice to be able to identify substances in this way. Keep reinforcing, with practical examples, that liquids pour but solids do not – don't confuse the issue with grains of salt or sugar!

The juice changes state – from a liquid to a solid – when it is frozen. Obviously, you are not going to tell your child that the juice has 'changed state' – but you should point out that the juice has changed from a liquid to a solid.

Boosting activity

Make an ice bowl with your child to emphasise that a liquid can be made into a solid by freezing. Make the bowl by half filling a six-litre plastic bowl with water, and placing a three-litre plastic bowl inside it. Hold the smaller bowl down in the larger bowl by using freezer tape across the top of both bowls, and then put the bowls in the freezer. You can add raspberries or herb leaves to the water between the bowls to make the ice bowl pretty.

58 Make chocolate spoons

This activity will boost your child's scientific knowledge and help him develop some practical skills. Carrying out the activity will help your child to learn about reversible changes, i.e. what happens when chocolate is heated and cooled, and may strengthen his interest in investigational work. Explaining the changes taking place will help your child to develop his own ideas.

Making the hot chocolate drink is a good conclusion to the activity as it reinforces the ideas learned; this is an effective way of making sure the ideas discussed are assimilated.

Boosting activity

Coat some soft fruit such as strawberries or raspberries with melted chocolate. You could also make chocolate shapes by pouring melted chocolate into moulds.

59 Learn about feelings

This activity is about building emotional literacy and intelligence. The activity will give your child the vocabulary to talk about how she feels – an essential life skill. Young children often feel very strong emotions but are not capable of putting them into words.

The discussion will also help your child to develop thinking skills as she describes the faces and the feelings she exhibits. The vocabulary building aspect of her language skills.

Acting out the feelings and body language will help your child to develop physical confidence. It also will ready your child for drama and acting activities. The collage activity will enable your child to practise cutting and sticking, an early art and technology skill.

Boosting activity

Offer your child poster paints and large pieces of paper so she can paint faces with different expressions. Cut the pictures out when they are dry, and write labels with a marker pen. Your child can then match the labels to the pictures.

60 Express how you feel

Playing 'Simon Says' will help your child to develop listening skills – imperative for all areas of learning. Using his whole body will help your child to feel physically comfortable when performing, and it will build confidence. This activity also will help your child to interpret people's emotions, which is an important life skill.

Making the food itself is an adventure in food technology. Your child will have to wash his hands, and think about hygiene; he will spread the cheese or peanut butter on the crackers, and will explore the textures and appearance of the food he chooses as different 'features' on the faces. Describing the emotions the faces represent will help your child to be articulate, developing her language skills.

Boosting activity

Start a loose-leaf folder recipe book for your child, and ask him to draw the faces he has made and label the ingredients used with leader lines and descriptions. Your child also can write up the 'method' used. This can be added to as and when as your child cooks food. it is a useful reminder of how to make the food and an example of non-fiction 'writing for a purpose'.

61 Make a friendship chain

This activity will help your child to think about what friendship means to her – and what it means to be a good friend, which is an important life skill.

Making the chain requires art and technology skills. Your child will be joining the strips to make circles and linking them together to make a chain. Writing the names on the links will encourage the neat formation of letters. Your child may have to copy the names from your writing. This activity also encourages the development of concentration as your child joins the links together to make the chain, which is quite complex for a child of this age.

Boosting activity

Your child could think about extended family members who do not live nearby, such as grandparents, and make small chains to send to them in a card labelled 'linked by love'. The chain could start with links named for the grandparents, then mother or father, and then add the child and any siblings. Your child could decorate the chain with glitter pens, drawing hearts and pictures of the family together.

62 Create a friendship circle

Talking about friends and the notion of what makes a friend will develop your child's ideas in the area of social and personal development. Speaking and listening will develop his ability to discuss matters.

Making the hands to create the rays of the sun will encourage him to work carefully, drawing round his hand. The cutting out may also be challenging; the activity will help your child to develop his coordination and fine motor skills.

Boosting activity

Have your child make a card for a friend, writing inside what it is that makes him such a good friend. Put a photo of the two children together on the front, or your child can draw a picture of them both together. This would make a lovely 'get-well' card for a friend who is sick.

63 Jobs people do

Young children have very vague ideas about what their parents do all day. Ask your child to tell you her ideas – you may be amazed! Talking to your child about the tasks you do at work, when you are apart, will give her a clearer picture in her mind's eye, and that will help your child to feel more secure when you are apart.

The world of work is something children find hard to understand. They need to learn about it by drip feeding rather than lots of information at once, so chat about your day with your child as well as asking about her school day.

Creating a fact file will help your child to develop a research habit where she organises facts and ideas into an easily readable form. Obviously at this stage your child's efforts will be very simple, but you are introducing her to the process.

Boosting activity

Try to arrange for your child to visit someone who has a job in which she is interested – fire stations, for example, often have open days when children can visit and see appliances, work equipment, etc. Take lots of photos and your child can make a book about her visit.

64 People who help us

This activity will help your child to think about the world of work, and the people in it. It will boost your child's language abilities as it requires your child to talk about the job that interests him most. 'Talking and listening' is an area in which teachers in schools often find that children need lots of practice. Making the book will also boost a child's literacy skills.

The activity will also stimulate your child's imagination, as he takes on and explores the job he has chosen through roleplay. Using the computer to manipulate text, clipart and photos will help your child to develop information technology skills; searching the Internet for information will develop your child's research skills.

Boosting activity

Have your child interview family members about their jobs. Retired grandparents may be particularly interesting to interview, especially if their jobs reflected an aspect of times past, i.e. a member of a typing pool.

Learn the parts of a plant

What you need

- A weed, such as a daisy, dug up from the garden or street. Wash the soil off the root
- For 'making' a plant: yellow, green and orange pieces of felt, brown thread, and a felt board
- Your make-and-glue kit

1 Find out what your child already knows about plants. Say something along the lines of: 'Look at this plant I dug up from the garden. Do you know what the parts of the plant are called?'

Explain which parts are the leaf, root, stem and flower. Talk simply about what job each part does (see picture).

2 Encourage your child to examine the plant, and to take it apart if he wishes. You could go outdoors or to the park at this point to look at other plants and see if your child can identify their parts.

Lastly, ask your child to make a felt model of a plant. He can cut out leaf, stem and flower onto the felt board using thread for the roots.

Flower attracts insects so they visit and pollinate the plant

Stem holds the flower up in the air so insects can visit, or the wind can catch the pollen

Root takes water and nutrients from the soil; helps hold the plant in the soil so it doesn't blow away

Leaf makes food like a special factory using sunlight

3 Go over what your child has learned. Can he remember what the parts of the plant are called and what their jobs are?

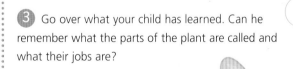

Stem

Petals

Leaves

Discover where bugs live

What you need

- Insect identification book: make sure it details the ones in your area
- White plastic tub (from ice cream or butter)
- Bug box or clear plastic pot
- Magnifier
- Your make-and-glue kit

1 Together with your child, look through a 'bug book'. Talk about the creatures that live in the gardens and parks where you live.

Tell your child you are going to go on a bug hunt. Ask her where you should look; this will help you to find out what your child already knows. It is always important to start where your children are. Ask your child to draw a picture of the garden or park where you are going to search. Your child can draw the creatures in the places where she expects to find them.

2 Go outdoors and look in the places your child has suggested as possible places for bugs – under stones, on leaves, etc. Talk about the reasons why bugs are found in the places they are. For example, caterpillars and beetles may be found on lettuces and other food plants, and ladybirds will be found on roses and beans where aphids abound.

You also may come across some worms in damp leaf litter or soil, and this will give you a chance to talk about the needs of most bugs (darkness, dampness and safety from predators).

Gently examine the bugs, picking them up with the hairs on a paintbrush and looking at them closely with the magnifier. What can you see? Point out antennae, legs and eyes.

3 Reinforce what your child has learned. Ask your child to look at the picture she drew before going outside. Were there any surprises?

Making a 'lift-the-flap' picture or book will help consolidate your child's learning (*see page 20*). Have her draw the bugs she found on a piece of paper, adding some background. Then she should cut out paper in the shapes of leaves, stones, soil, etc., to stick as a flap over each creature to show where it was found.

1 Look at the books together to find pictures of aquaria. Visit the aquarium or pet shop/garden centre to look at aquaria. Talk with your child about the way they are made — the materials you can see, and why they have been used, etc.

Look closely at the inhabitants of the aquaria together, discussing their characteristics, such as legs (if any), antennae, skin texture, fins, etc.

What you need

- Visit to aquarium or pet shop/garden centre that sells fish
- Books for children about keeping an aquarium
- Cardboard box or carton – slightly larger than a shoe box
- Scrap card
- Foil sweet wrappers
- Dark thread
- Clear green cellophane/crêpe paper/plastic cut from a food bag
- Your make-and-glue kit
- Blue and green paint
- Paintbrush
- Glitter
- Brown plasticine or clay
- Pulses such as mung beans, green lentils etc.

2 Help your child to cut rectangles out of three sides of the box (the front and the two short sides) to make windows for the aquarium. Paint the frame you are left with, inside and out. When it is dry, cover the windows with cellophane taped inside the box. Cut the lid off the box completely. You now have your basic aquarium.

Coat the bottom of the inside of your aquarium with glue and cover the glue in pulses to create a sandy, rocky effect. Cut thin strips of card, and tape them across the top of your aquarium to hang creatures from.

Aquatic creatures such as shrimp, anemones, fish, etc., can be made using the books as a guide.

The creatures need lengths of dark thread taped to them. The other end of the tape should be taped to the strips across the top of the box so that it looks as though the creatures are swimming in the aquarium. Make weed with green cellophane/crêpe paper and stick it to the back of the aquarium. Add a few rocks made from brown plasticine and your aquarium is finished.

3 Ask your child to explain how she made the aquarium. Can she tell people about the creatures she made – how they act, and what they eat, for example – from the research she did before she started making them?

Go pond dipping

What you need

- Small net
- White plastic food-packaging tray
- Clear plastic pot
- Field guide to pond life
- Magnifier
- Rubber boots
- Camera

① Tell your child you are going to go pond dipping. Ask him which creatures he expects to see in and around the pond. Look at the field guide together and identify likely creatures.

② Wearing rubber boots, visit a pond. Ponds in some parks may have jetties that take you over the water; they may also have interpretation boards with pictures of creatures you are likely to see.

Explain the importance of safety to your child, and that he should not come pond dipping without a responsible adult.

Scoop the net through weed and at the margins of the pool. Gently empty finds into the white tray and try to identify them. Take photographs to look at later. Look at particularly interesting finds with the magnifier.

Make sure you look at and discuss the plants you can see in and around the pond. Are they different to plants found away from water? Look for signs of mammals and birds around the margins of the pond – has anything been feeding, or can you see any footprints in the mud? Look at bugs flying above the water, too, paying special attention to creatures that spend part of their lifecycle in the water, such as dragonflies and damselflies.

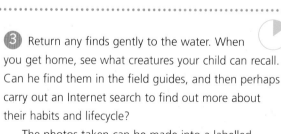

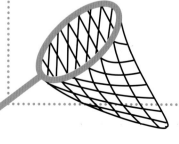

③ Return any finds gently to the water. When you get home, see what creatures your child can recall. Can he find them in the field guides, and then perhaps carry out an Internet search to find out more about their habits and lifecycle?

The photos taken can be made into a labelled display or mounted to make a memories book about the day.

Sensory woodland walk

What you need

- Books about trees and woodland life
- Binoculars
- Magnifier
- Soft toy or glove puppet of a local woodland animal
- Paper bag for 'finds'
- Wax crayons
- Paper
- Cardboard box

1 Look at the books together and talk about what you might see on a walk in the woods. Encourage your child to offer suggestions. Be prepared for some surprising ideas!

2 Go out into accessible woods. Small children find woodland walking easier in woodlands with paths.

Take the binoculars, magnifier, paper and wax crayon with you. Encourage your child to breathe in the woodland smells, and talk about the colours and textures you both see. Let her feel the leaves and tell her about the veins being tiny tubes that carry water and goodness around the plant.

Look at objects through the magnifier, and encourage your child to describe what she sees. Use the binoculars to look closely at birds and the tree canopy.

Use the paper and the side of the wax crayons to take various bark rubbings. Hold the paper securely while your child does the rubbing.

Talk about the cuddly toy you have chosen. What would it eat? Where would it sleep? Can you find any clues that your chosen animal has been nearby e.g. nibbled nuts, chewed pine cones, tufts of hair, footprints, or droppings?

Collect leaves and twigs to take home.

3 Back at home, talk about what you have seen. Look at the bark rubbings and ask your child how the bark felt. Build a nest for the cuddly toy out of the leaves and twigs.

Compile a leaf diary

What you need

- Resource material on seasonal change
- Notebook or scrapbook
- Watercolours, brush and palette
- Your make-and-glue kit
- Camera

1 Talk about the way that leaves of some trees change colour from green through yellow, orange and red. Ask your child if he can explain why, in simple terms. Tell him that you are going to find out more together.

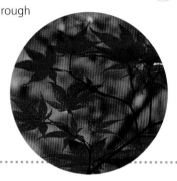

2 Encourage your child to find out more about why leaves change colour in the autumn by looking in books and on websites. Basically, the tree shuts down the leaves as 'food factories' as the days grow shorter and light levels fall. The leaves change colour as the tree re-absorbs the chlorophyll – the green colouring – that it uses to make food in the leaves via sunlight.

The yellow, orange and red colours are always present in the leaves, but are masked during the warmer months by the green colouring.

Once the tree has re-absorbed the chlorophyll, the leaves fall to the ground, ready for new leaves to grow in the spring.

Go outside with your child in the autumn, choosing a tree to watch. Every few days, your child should take a picture of the tree as the colours change and try to replicate the colours of collected leaves by colour mixing.

The photo, collected leaves, colour mixing and any comments your child wishes to include can be stuck into the scrapbook and a tree diary cover made.

3 Ask your child to explain what has happened to the tree as time passes. Can he predict how quickly the leaves will change colour, and how long it will be before the last leaf falls?

Create a window box farm

What you need

- Fresh or tinned food marked with country of origin labels or stickers
- Atlas or globe
- Window box or pots filled with compost
- Lettuce and radish seeds
- Watering can

1 Talk to your child about where food comes from. If she says 'the shops', ask her where the shops get the food. Talk about how the food we eat is grown or farmed by someone – even if food is processed (say 'made into another kind of food') such as wheat being ground into flour and made into bread. Look at the stickers and labels on the food to find the countries that produced them. Use the globe or atlas to locate some of the countries.

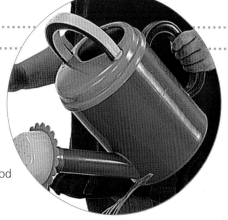

2 Now tell your child you are going to 'farm' some food together. Plant the seeds in the compost and water them. Make sure the window box or pots are in the sun. Lettuce and radish seeds germinate within days and grow to maturity quickly, so your child will see results very soon. Make sure you 'harvest' and eat the food with due ceremony!

3 Talk about all the people we rely upon around the world for our food. Try to arrange a visit to a 'pick-your-own' farm or a local smallholding or allotment garden to see food being produced.

Construct a seasons mobile

What you need

- Rectangular card or stiff paper, about 60 cm long
- Crêpe paper
- String or wool
- Paint
- Paint brush
- Your make-and-glue kit

① Talk about the seasons. What makes your child think about each season? Prompt him with the events that take place during each season, such as Halloween, Christmas, Easter and summer holidays.

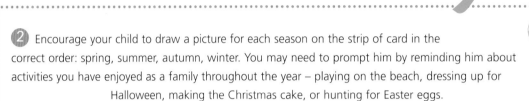

② Encourage your child to draw a picture for each season on the strip of card in the correct order: spring, summer, autumn, winter. You may need to prompt him by reminding him about activities you have enjoyed as a family throughout the year – playing on the beach, dressing up for Halloween, making the Christmas cake, or hunting for Easter eggs.

Tape together the two short ends of the card to make a tube. Cut thin strips of crêpe paper and tape them inside the bottom of the tube, so they dangle like ribbons. Tape a length of string or wool to the top of the tube to make a 'handle' and hang up the mobile.

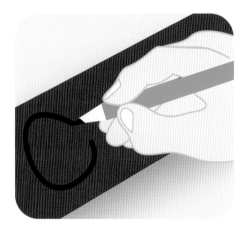

③ Ask your child to explain which season is which, and why he drew the pictures he did for each season. Could he name three things that make him think of each season?

Make a starfish badge

39

What you need

- Resource material about starfish
- A dry or model starfish
- Scrap card
- Your make-and-glue kit
- Birdseed or rough oatmeal
- Orange and green paint
- Paintbrush
- Glitter
- Safety pin

1 Talk about the last time you saw a starfish. What did it look like? Recall a visit to the aquarium or look at pictures on websites and books. Find out about the starfish – it has some amazing attributes, such as being able to grow a new leg if one is damaged, or being able to pass its stomach out through its mouth to digest shellfish! Talk about the texture of a starfish. If you have a dried or model starfish, encourage your child to explore it with his skin. Talk about its appearance, such as having five legs and a rough skin.

2 Cut a starfish shape from the card to make the badge. Tape the safety pin securely to the back of the badge. Encourage your child to spread glue on the front of the badge, and then sprinkle on the oatmeal/birdseed. When the glue is dry, he should paint the badge orange, and add flecks of green.

When the badge is dry, have him add blobs of glue and sprinkle on a little glitter. When the blobs of glue are dry, your child should coat the front of the badge in a thick layer of white PVA glue. When it dries, it will be clear, and look wet. This strong shiny coating also helps to keep the decorations on the badge.

3 Ask your child to explain to another family member how he made his badge, pointing out which parts were the most difficult to do.

Create a dinosaur puppet

What you need

- Card
- Small coin
- Books about dinosaurs
- Collage materials of different textures to decorate the puppet
- Your make-and-glue kit

1 Tell your child he can make a dinosaur finger puppet, but first find out what he already knows about dinosaurs: 'Can you tell me about a stegosaurus or a tyrannosaurus? What colour do you think it was? What do you think it ate?'

Then look through the books together. When your child spots the relevant dinosaur, read the text to him. Build up a 'fact file' about the dinosaur(s) you are investigating.

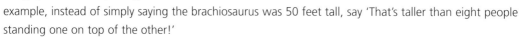
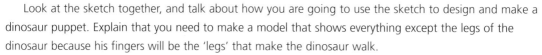

2 Encourage your child to make a large sketch of his chosen dinosaur. Talk about how long the neck needs to be; how tall the dinosaur is. Compare sizes to things your child may recognize. For example, instead of simply saying the brachiosaurus was 50 feet tall, say 'That's taller than eight people standing one on top of the other!'

Look at the sketch together, and talk about how you are going to use the sketch to design and make a dinosaur puppet. Explain that you need to make a model that shows everything except the legs of the dinosaur because his fingers will be the 'legs' that make the dinosaur walk.

Talk about the materials you will use to make the puppet. What are they like? Are they soft, hard, stiff, bendy, etc. This gives your child design and technology vocabulary that he will use later on in school.

Help your child to draw his dinosaur shape onto card, including drawing round the coin in the correct position to make 'leg holes'. When the dinosaur is decorated, your child may need help cutting it out.

3 How did it go? Would your child do anything differently next time? What parts was he pleased with? Then ask him to put on a show with his dinosaur puppet. But be warned, he may want to make extra characters ... and a backdrop ...

Make a dinosaur mobile

What you need

- Reference material about dinosaurs
- Card
- Green crêpe paper
- Paints or felt pens
- Your make-and-glue kit
- Thread

1 Look through books and at websites together and encourage your child to choose four dinosaurs he finds interesting. Talk about the shape of the dinosaurs. Do they have long necks, tails, spines, neck frills or horns? What size were the dinosaurs he has chosen, relative to each other?

2 Your child should draw 'his' dinosaurs on card and colour or paint them. The dinosaurs should be cut out, and pieces of thread of different lengths attached to the back of the shapes with tape.

Your child should cut a circle from card from which to hang the dinosaurs. This can be covered with green crêpe paper, or painted green to make a jungle effect. Strips of crêpe paper can be cut and gently stretched between finger and thumb to make foliage fronds that can also be taped on to the card circle for effect.

Attach a single thread to the top of the circle to suspend it from the ceiling.

3 Talk together about what your child has done. Were some parts of making the mobile harder than others? Would your child change anything about the process if he made something similar?

Your child could use the mobile in a 'show and tell' exercise, to inform family or friends about the dinosaurs he included in his model. Did your child learn anything new about these particular dinosaurs in the course of his research?

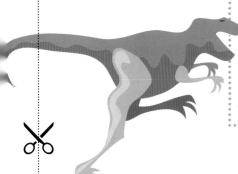

Hatch some dinosaur eggs

1 Look through the books about dinosaurs, checking for information about egg laying. Encourage your child to find pictures of nests and young hatching from eggs. Talk about the size of the babies compared to the adult dinosaurs. What evidence is there for dinosaurs laying eggs?

What you need

- Books about dinosaurs
- 1 cup of flour
- 1 cup of coffee grounds
- ½ cup of salt
- ¼ cup of play sand
- 1 cup of water
- Small plastic dinosaur toys
- Bowl
- Wooden spoon

2 Have your child mix the dry ingredients together in a bowl then add the water. She should work the resulting 'clay' to make it pliable.

Your child should mould a hollow 'half egg' shape from the 'clay', place a dinosaur inside, and mould a second half. The two halves should be combined to make a whole egg shape. She should repeat until the mixture or dinosaurs run out. Leave the eggs to dry for around 3–4 days. The texture will be gritty and 'realistic'. If your child is keen, she may like to make a 'nest' for the eggs from crumpled brown paper.

3 Talk together about what your child has done. After 3–4 days, your child can crack the eggs to 'hatch' the dinosaurs! If she has a younger brother or sister she may like to make the 'hatching' a theatrical affair, embellishing the event with the story of the discovery of the nest … and even the return of the parent dinosaur!

Stock a story chest

1 Paint the box brown, and when it's dry, stick strips of black paper onto it to look like leather straps. Add silver 'rivets' here and there with the gel pen. Make some buckles from card and glue on the ends. Ask your child what things could go into the box and used to tell a story about a castle in which a princess, knight, king or dragon, lives. Look for items in your child's toy box, or make paper crowns and necklaces and cardboard swords and daggers.

Shoe box

Strips of black paper to look like leather straps

Silver 'rivets'

Buckles

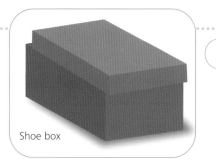

What you need

- Cardboard box with a lid, such as large shoe box
- Brown paint
- Black paper
- Silver gel pen
- Yellow card (or plain card coloured yellow)
- Items on the theme to fill box such as toy sword, dragon model, crown, necklace, rings, wand, toy knights or wizards, etc.
- Your make-and-glue kit

2 Ask your child to take things out of the story chest, one at a time, and help him to make up a story about life in the castle, prompted by each item. Will the dragon be fierce or cowardly? Will she be a fire dragon or an ice dragon? Will the princess be strong and brave or mean and nasty? Will the knight be a mighty dragon slayer or a wimp? Try to encourage your child to use lots of descriptive words: Not just 'a dragon', but 'a fierce, scaly dragon'.

3 Encourage your child to repeat his stories to family and friends. Ask him which were the most exciting parts. You could even make a book together to remember the story, adding drawings by your child to the pages (you can act as 'scribe' and write down his story) and add a photograph of your child telling the story – like an author's picture – on the back of his book.

Make a mermaid/merman

What you need

- Pictures or books about mermaids/mermen
- Roll of lining paper
- Wool
- Sequins
- Green and flesh-tone paint
- Glitter
- Small shells
- Paintbrushes
- Your make-and-glue kit

1 Look at the books and pictures. If possible, tell a story about mer people. Unroll the lining paper and ask your child to lie down on the paper with his legs together — his shape will make the tail! Draw round your child to make the outline of the mermaid or man.

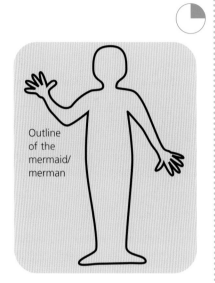

Outline of the mermaid/ merman

2 Talk about how mermaids and men look in stories. Help your child to paint the head, arms and body of the mermaid or man. Use the collage materials to create a sparkling tail. Stick on wool scraps as hair and add shells. Ask your child to describe where his mermaid/merman might live.

Stick on wool scraps as hair

Add shells

Use the collage materials to create a sparkling tail

3 Ask your child to tell you about mermaids/mermen. What can he remember about your story?

What you need

- Resource material on pirates
- Cardboard tubes (such as toilet tissue inner tubes)
- Paper
- Your make-and-glue kit

1 Look at your resource material and talk about what pirates looked like. Point out hats, eye patches, stripy tops and scars. Ask your child to describe a variety of pirates, including a captain, a female pirate, and even the ship's cat and a parrot.

2 Each cardboard tube will be the head and body of a pirate. They can be coloured in accordingly, with stripy shirts, dark – or ragged – trousers, and even a wooden leg.

On separate small pieces of paper, your child can draw hats and hands. He might need help to cut them out and stick them to the tubes to complete the pirates.

A cat can be made in the same way, colouring the body but cutting out a ears, limbs and tail from paper. A parrot may be made by colouring the body, then adding a tail and wings cut from paper and coloured brightly. If your child is really keen, he can make palm trees in the same way: the tube is the trunk, and green paper (or even green feathers) pushed into the top become the palm fronds. The background can be as simple as a yellow scarf or piece of paper for the 'treasure island' and a blue piece for the sea.

3 Your child can now make up adventures for the pirates. It may be fun to video or photograph your child's play to look at together later.

Fly a jolly roger

① Look at books, magazines and DVDs for images of the pirate flag – the skull and cross bones. Tell your child it is called a 'Jolly Roger', and that sailors were very afraid when they saw it flying above a ship because they knew they were about to get attacked and robbed! Tell your child she is going to make a Jolly Roger of her own.

What you need

- Resource material on pirates
- Black cotton scarf or rectangular piece of black material
- Tracing paper
- White card
- Your make-and-glue kit

JOLLY ROGER TEMPLATE

Enlarge as desired

② Transfer the template to graph paper to enlarge, or use a photocopier. Then have your child cut it out and transfer it to the white card by drawing round the edges. She should then cut round the whole shape and remove the eyes, nose and mouth.

Stick the skull and crossbones in the middle of the black material.

③ Attach the flag to the wall – or the end of the sofa! Pretend to be pirates aboard ship! If you have some dressing-up items you can use to make yourselves into pirates, so much the better …

Create a captain's cutlass

What you need

- Resource material about pirates
- Rigid cardboard box
- Thinner scrap card
- Grey paint
- Black marker pen
- Gold glitter
- Sequins or beads
- Your make-and-glue kit

1 Talk about the weapons a pirate may have carried. Look at books and websites to find pictures of a cutlass. Talk about how it would have been held and used.

CUTLASS TEMPLATE

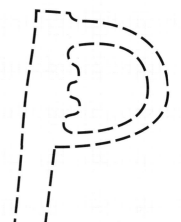

2 Transfer the template onto graph paper to enlarge or use a photocopier. Then use the new template to cut two blade pieces from the cardboard box. Glue the pieces together to make a stiff, strong blade. Paint this piece grey and, once the paint is dry, draw two vertical lines down the blade with the marker to make it look 3D.

Cut an oval shape from the thinner card and make two slits, as shown on the bottom template. Push the handle of the blade through the slits, bending the card to make a hand shield, and glue it into place.

Decorate the hand shield part of the cutlass with gold glitter. Then glue on a few sequins or beads as jewels.

Cut an oval shape from the thinner card and make two slits

3 When the cutlass is dry, ask your child if he can write a list of instructions to show someone else how to make a cutlass. Can he use what he has learned to adapt the plan and make a longer pirate sword?

Enlarge these shapes as desired

Make a pirate boot clip

What you need

- Resource material about pirates
- White card
- Felt pens
- Your make-and-glue kit
- Contact sticky plastic sheet or a laminator
- Wooden clothes pegs

1 Talk about the clothes pirates wore. Were the captains dressed differently to the ordinary pirates? What did female pirates wear? Look at books and websites to find pictures. Tell your child she is going to make a pirate welly boot holder – because all pirates need to keep their boots organised!

2 Your child should draw a picture of a pirate onto the card. She should colour it in bright colours and cover it in plastic (or laminate it). Then she should cut it out and glue it to the peg. You could make different characters for the whole family!

3 Ask your child to write a list of instructions to tell someone else how to make a clip. Can she adapt the plan and make clips with other themes to give as gifts?

Capture a fairy!

What you need

- Resource material on fairies
- Clean, empty jam jar
- Modelling clay
- Card
- Glitter
- Your make-and-glue kit

① Look at books and/or internet sites about fairies together. Talk about what fairies are supposed to be like, according to stories and legends. You could even talk about Tinkerbell or the tooth fairy!

② Talk about what it would be like if you found fairies in a garden. Look for details of the Cottingley case of 1912, where little girls discovered fairies in the garden, which were actually photographed.

Tell your child she is going to make a captured fairy. Your child should make a fairy from modelling clay. Then she should cut a wand and wings from card and cover them in glitter. These should be pushed into the model.

Take the lid off the jam jar, and place the jar upside down. The fairy should be placed on the lid, using a little wet clay to secure it, then the jar should be put on top, so that the fairy is held inside it.

Have your child make a label for the jar, with the fairy's name, and the date and place of capture!

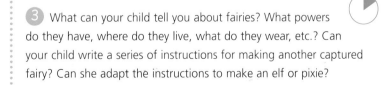

③ What can your child tell you about fairies? What powers do they have, where do they live, what do they wear, etc.? Can your child write a series of instructions for making another captured fairy? Can she adapt the instructions to make an elf or pixie?

1. Introduce the subject of ancient times and people. Talk in simple terms about pyramids, mummies and desert scenes. Look in brochures, magazines and books, and on websites for images of the ancient Egyptians and talk about how different life was in these times.

What you need

- Resource material on ancient Egypt
- Play sand
- Your make-and-glue kit

2. Ask your child to select images he'd like to use in a sand picture. Help him to cut out photographs or download them from the Internet.

Ask your child to spread glue on a sheet of paper and sprinkle sand all over the surface. After shaking off the excess sand, your child can glue the photographs onto the sand to make an Egyptian scene. He could sprinkle extra sand on top to make it appear as if they were about to be discovered!

3. Ask your child to tell you about his picture. Which photographs did he choose and why? What can he tell you about life in ancient Egypt?

Plan an expedition to a local museum to look at Egyptian displays and artefacts, and find out more.

Make a mummy book

What you need

- Resource materials about ancient Egypt and mummies
- Card
- White tissue paper
- Metallic sweet wrappers
- Sequins
- Stapler
- Your make-and-glue kit

1 Share books and visit websites, looking at mummies and how and why they were made. Talk in simple terms about what the ancient Egyptians believed about life after death, and why they buried people with treasure and other items. Make sure you look at special tomb discoveries such as that of Tutankhamun.

MUMMY TEMPLATE

Enlarge as desired

2 Using graph paper or a photocopier, enlarge the shape opposite as necessary and make a template. Help your child to transfer the shape onto three pieces of card then cut each out. On the bottom layer, your child should draw an ancient Egyptian person. On the middle layer, she should construct the mummy by gluing pieces of tissue paper to the shape. To make it look more 'wrapped', she could draw 'bandage lines' on the tissue once it is dry.

The top layer should be made to look like a sarcophagus, and be highly decorated with sweet wrappers and sequins. When all three layers are dry, staple them together at one edge.

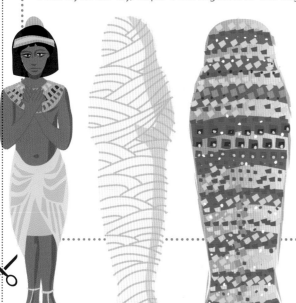

3 What can your child tell you about how and why mummies were made, using her book as a prompt?

Model an Egyptian mask

What you need

- Resource material on ancient Egypt
- Thick card, from a packaging box
- Gold and metallic blue paint OR gold and metallic blue paper
- Newspaper
- Your make-and-glue kit
- Large lump of plasticine or similar modelling clay
- Mirror
- Black marker pen

1 Share books and visit websites, looking at the masks created by ancient Egyptians and found in their tombs. Talk about what these death masks were for, and who would have had them. Look at the pharaoh Tutankhamun's mask, which is a particularly beautiful example. If possible, visit a museum to look at some or, if you've been previously, remind your child about what you saw.

2 Transfer the template to graph paper to enlarge or use a photocopier. Transfer it to the card and cut it out. Encourage your child to look in the mirror at the shape of her face, and to mould the plasticine into a face. She should press the plasticine face onto the cardboard and cover both the face and card with newspaper strips and glue until it is four layers thick. Once it is dry, your child should paint the model gold and add decoration with blue paint. Alternatively, cover the model with pieces of gold and blue paper to make a pattern. Add details such as eyes and nostrils with a black marker pen.

TEMPLATE FOR DEATH MASK

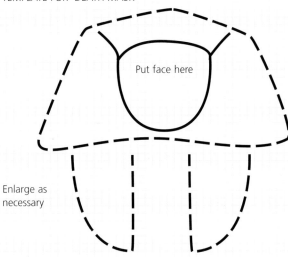

Put face here

Enlarge as necessary

3 Ask your child to explain how she made the death mask, Can she use the mask to give a presentation about how and why death masks were made in ancient Egypt?

Let's go exploring

What you need

- Fabric (tablecloths, sheets or curtains)
- Cushions
- Maps, hat, bag, compass and toy binoculars for 'props'
- Children's atlas
- Photographs of wild, beautiful places
- A drink and edible 'supplies'

1 Build a base camp for your child using the fabric. This can be as simple as draping the material between the backs of two chairs or over a small table. Lay the cushions and props inside the den. Explain to your child that you are going to play at being explorers.

2 To fire your child's imagination, talk about the quest you are going on. Look at photographs in travel brochures and the atlas. What sort of country will you explore? Will it be hot or cold? Will it have jungles and deserts or mountains and waterfalls? What are the animals like? Will you meet any people on your expedition? What will you need for the journey? Use the props to pack a bag, talking about what you will use each item for as you pack it.

Now travel together around the house and garden, talking about the things you 'see' in your imagination. Are you wading through a swamp – and is that a fierce crocodile? Is the mountain hard to climb – and can you see that eagle in the sky? Add lots of details so your child will get the idea and add his, too!

3 Sit down and talk about your 'journey'. What can your child remember? How would it feel to be a real explorer? Talk about feeling excited and scared. Then eat your snack. If it is exotic fruit, talk about where it came from, and look for the country in the atlas.

Map a 'lost' city

What you need

- Children's atlas
- Large sheet of white paper
- Candle
- Brown paint
- Paintbrush
- Scraps of metallic sweet wrappers
- Red ribbon
- Red modelling clay
- Your make-and-glue kit

1 Talk to your child about maps and what they are used for. Look at the atlas and talk about where you live. Discuss with your child the rivers, mountains, railways, etc., she can see in the atlas. Then tell your child that you are both going to look for the Lost City of Zargar! But first, you must make a map. Use your imagination – and fire your child's – by describing the city. Make it as wild and exciting as you can. Who lives there? Sparkly blue frost giants? Or fire beasts with burning eyes? What are the buildings like? Are they made from mauve crystal or liquid metal that reflects the sky? What do the creatures that live there eat? Build a word picture of the place together.

2 Before your child can start making the map, you must prepare the large piece of paper by burning the edges with a candle for an authentic 'aged' effect. Meanwhile, ask your child to make a pot of thin, watery brown paint and to paint both sides of the map – not too thick, remember, you need to be able to see the features of the map when they are added.

When the paper is dry, encourage your child to draw features such as rivers, mountains, deserts, jungles and swamps. Ask her to cut the sweet wrappers into shapes and stick them on the map to make a glittering city. Finally, encourage your child to make an 'official seal' for the bottom of the map. Glue two short strips of ribbon onto the map. Mold a piece of red clay into a ball and press a coin against the ball to make an impression, then glue the resulting disc onto the ribbon to make the seal.

3 Talk about the map, and ask your child to recount the steps she took to make it. Can she remember what the features on the map represent? Play with the map: add some treasure to be found in the City of Zargar and make it into a treasure hunt – perhaps the sweets that came out of the wrappers?

Learn about wind power

What you need

- Toy windmill
- Bubble liquid and blower
- Two sheets of newspaper
- Your make-and-glue kit

1 Go outside with your child on a windy day. Talk about what is happening. Can your child see the effect of the wind? Are the trees swaying? Is the wind strong enough for your child to feel a 'push' against her as she walks along? Is her hair blowing in the breeze? Are the clouds moving quickly across the sky? Point out any visible effects of the wind blowing.

2 Talk to your child about the power of air and how it makes things happen.

Use the bubble blower to blow bubbles together, pointing out that it is your breath – the moving air – that makes bubbles from the soapy liquid. Blow on the windmill together, and talk about how your breath or air moves it.

Make a game to demonstrate the power of moving air. Cut two cloud shapes from a sheet of paper. Place the cloud shapes on the floor and have a race. You each need a some newspaper to waft the clouds across the floor. Ask your child: 'Does it make a difference if you waft your cloud quickly?'

Waft the clouds across the floor

3 Reinforce the idea that moving air is powerful and can make things move. Go over what you saw outside and the effect that flapping the newspaper had on the 'clouds'.

Does it float or sink?

① Talk about floating and sinking. Check that your child knows what the words mean. Ask him to tell you what sort of things float, giving examples. Encourage him to talk about bath toys and other familiar objects such as swimming floats and sailboats.

What you need

- Variety of objects that float or sink such as: bath toys, cork, plastic cup, coin, stone, empty ice cream tub, key, apple, cotton wool ball, shell, plastic ball
- Washing-up bowl full of water
- Pens
- Paper with two circles drawn on, one labelled 'float', the other 'sink'

② Encourage your child to look carefully at the objects you have chosen. Ask him to predict which ones will float and which will sink. He can record his predictions as drawings on the appropriate circle. Then test each item in turn. Were your child's predictions correct?

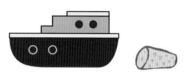

float

sink

③ Discuss with your child why he made his decisions – it is likely he will say that light things float and heavy things sink. Tell him that this is quite a good clue, but it is not always the case. Point out that huge ships, made from metal, float – and they are very heavy. It would be interesting to see whether your child's predictions are materially different if you repeat the exercise with different objects.

Turn a liquid to a solid

1 Have a drink of the fruit juice. Talk to your child about the juice, how it is a liquid rather than solid, and ask her to explore and describe it. Say something like 'What happens if I tilt my glass to one side?' or 'Is this set like jelly or runny like water?'

Can your child think of any other liquids? You could search the kitchen looking for some, such as milk or lemonade.

What you need

- Fruit juice
- Ice lolly mould, or plastic cup
- Ice cubes

2 Ask your child how a fruit ice lolly is different from fruit juice (you are looking for the answer that it is solid, and will not pour). Fill the ice lolly mould or plastic cup with fruit juice and put it in the freezer. When the juice has frozen, take the lolly out of the freezer for your child to sample. Point out that the juice has changed from a liquid to a solid.

Ask your child how the lolly could be changed from a solid back to a liquid. If she doesn't come up with a suggestion, prompt her by asking what happens to ice cream on a sunny day – and she will remember that it melts.

3 Demonstrate ice changing back into a liquid by taking some of the ice cubes from the freezer and leaving them in a warm place. Can your child think of any other foods that change from a liquid to a solid or vice versa? You could experiment with melting chocolate and creating different shapes with moulds.

Make chocolate spoons

What you need

- 2 chocolate bars
- Microwave oven
- 2 plastic disposable spoons
- Tray
- 2 cups of milk

1 Open one of the bars of chocolate and sample it together. Talk about the way it feels in your mouths – solid to start with, but melting as your mouth heats it up. Hold a piece in your fingers and watch it start to melt. As you wipe (or lick!) it away, again talk about the way heat – this time of your hand – has changed the chocolate from a solid to a liquid.

2 Melt the chocolate in the microwave. Ask your child to carefully stir the melted chocolate and to explain what has happened to the chocolate. He should be able to tell you that the heat has changed the chocolate, making it turn from a solid into a liquid. You and your child should each dip the bowl of a plastic spoon into the chocolate, coating them. Leave them on a tray until the chocolate has hardened. Ask your child to explain what changes the chocolate is undergoing as it cools.

3 Heat the milk and pour into two glasses; add a chocolate spoon to each. Stir the milk, and its colour will change from white to brown as the chocolate melts – you have made hot chocolate! But your child can earn his treat by telling you what has happened to change the chocolate …

While you are enjoying your drinks, take a virtual chocolate factory tour at the Cadbury's website: cadburyworld.co.uk

Learn about feelings

1 Look at the photos with your child. Ask him to describe the emotion each person is feeling and to suggest why the person is feeling that way. If he needs help, you can suggest one reason and ask him to provide another – 'He is sad because it is raining and he can't play outside ....'

What you need

- About 10 faces, cut from magazines, showing different expressions
- Mirror

2 Talk about the things that make you both feel happy, angry or excited – as many emotions as you can think of. Act out different feelings, using facial expressions as well as body language. Encourage your child to look in the mirror so he see his face as it changes.

3 Make a collage of the faces cut from the magazines. Afterwards, describe each emotion and ask your child to choose a face that represents it to check that he remembers the 'emotion words'.

sad

happy

scared angry

Express how you feel

What you need

- Round crackers
- Peanut butter or cream cheese
- Vegetables cut into thin strips and chunks
- Grapes
- Cherry tomatoes
- Sultanas

1 Play 'Simon says' – but with feelings rather than actions. So you say, 'Simon says, "Make a happy face",' etc., and your child responds accordingly. Make it a whole body experience too, by saying 'Simon says, "Walk round the room angrily."'

2 Now make 'feelings food'. Help your child to spread cheese or peanut butter onto the crackers. She should then make faces on the crackers using the cut-up vegetables and fruit. Can she tell you which feelings the faces represent?

3 Talk about how you can tell what feelings people are experiencing. Can your child describe how different emotions make her feel?

What you need

- Coloured paper
- Your make-and-glue kit

1 Ask your child to think about people she likes. They could be play group or school friends, neighbours or family members. Help her to make a list. You could use photographs or a photo album to jog her memory.

2 Encourage your child to draw a picture of each 'friend' on her list. Meanwhile, you cut the coloured paper into 2.5 x 10 cm strips. Ask your child (with your help) to write one name in the middle of each strip. Then link the strips together in loops, securing with tape, to make a chain. Hang the friendship chain in the kitchen or any other high-traffic area.

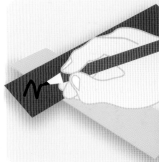

3 Look at the chain together, and encourage your child to say one thing she likes about each person on it. Then ask your child what she thinks it is that makes someone a friend. Is it the way the person acts and the things he or she does? As your child makes new friends, she can add new links.

What you need

- Yellow, orange and gold paper
- Yellow card
- Large piece white card
- A4 envelope
- Your make-and-glue kit

1 Talk to your child about his friends. Why are they friends? Do they have things in common? Do they like to do the same things? Are they kind to each other? What makes a good friend?

2 Cut a circle out of yellow card – you could use a plate as a template – and glue it centrally to a circle of white card, which extends out about 10 cm. Then ask your child to draw round his hand on the coloured papers about 20 times. Help him cut out his 'hands', then put them in a large envelope secured to the back of the board. Hang the circle or fix it to a wall. Each time a new friend visits or comes to play, this child should write his or her name and draw his or her face on a 'hand'. Your child can add the hands around the edge of the circle, with the fingers pointing outwards.

3 Ask your child to think about whether he is a good friend. What has he done for other people to make him a good friend? Can he think of more he can do to be a good friend?

Jobs people do

What you need

- Reference material about workers
- Magazines, newspapers and brochures
- Paper
- Your make-and-glue kit

1 Tell your child about your job, and the jobs of other people she knows. What jobs can she think of? Make a list together; your child may wish to draw pictures that you label for her.

2 Encourage your child to think about what people do as a part of their jobs. Look at books, magazines and websites together to find out more. Choose a job she is interested in and make a 'fact file' together. You could look on the Internet to find clipart and photographs for your child to print off and write captions for her file. Alternatively, cut pictures out of magazines.

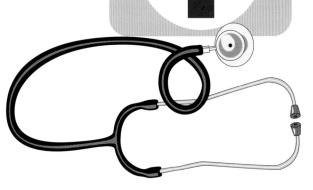

3 Talk about the new things you have found out about the jobs you have investigated. Encouraging your child to review knowledge will help her to retain it.

People who help us

What you need

- Reference material about different jobs
- Pictures of firefighters, police, nurses, doctors, teachers, crossing guards, dentists, etc.
- Paper
- Your make-and-glue kit
- Dressing up clothes or props

1 Ask your child to think about all the different types of people there are to help him. How many can he think of? Prompt your child with the pictures if he struggles. Use the images to make a collage.

2 Ask your child to choose a job to research. Look on the Internet or in books together to find more information. If possible, locate some items to help your child to dress up for his chosen 'job', or at least find some props such as a hose for a firefighter, a home-made sign for a crossing warden, a bag for a doctor, etc. Encourage your child to act in his role, and pretend to help him arrange his soft toys appropriately. A 'doctor' could put them in 'hospital beds', a 'teacher' could set them up in a 'classroom', etc. Join in to help your child to enter his imaginary role.

3 Encourage your child to tell you about what he has done in his role. He could make a simple book about the job he chose, perhaps using the computer to type out the text. Help him to drop clipart or photos from a source such as Google Images into his writing.

INDEX

ACKNOWLEDGEMENTS

Photographer Jules Selmes
Illustrator Mark Buckingham

Cover Image: imagesource
p14 BRIO toys
p15 imagesource
p25 imagesource
p41 imagesource

DATE	TEST/ACTIVITY	RESULTS/REMARKS